Junior
MasterChef
1998

Junior
MasterChef
1998

Foreword by Loyd Grossman

General Editor: Janet Illsley

EBURY PRESS
LONDON

1 3 5 7 9 10 8 6 4 2

Compilation copyright © Union Pictures 1998
Recipes copyright © The Contributors 1998
Foreword © Loyd Grossman 1998
Introduction © Richard Bryan 1998
Back cover photograph © Richard Farley 1998

First published in the United Kingdom in 1998 by Ebury Press,
Random House, 20 Vauxhall Bridge Road, London SW1V 2SA

Random House Australia (Pty) Limited
20 Alfred Street, Milsons Point, Sydney
New South Wales 2061, Australia

Random House New Zealand Limited
18 Poland Road, Glenfield
Auckland 10, New Zealand

Random House South Africa (Pty) Limited
Endulini, 5A Jubilee Road
Parktown 2193, South Africa

Random House UK Limited Reg. No. 954009

A CIP catalogue record for this book is available from the British Library

ISBN: 0 09 185322 2

Junior MasterChef 1998
A Union Pictures production for BBC North
Series devised by Franc Roddam
Executive Producers: Bradley Adams and Richard Kalms
Producer and Director: Richard Bryan
Associate Producer: Glynis Robertson
Production Co-ordinators: Julia Park and Katy Savage

General Editor: Janet Illsley
Design: Clive Dorman
Typeset in Garamond by Clive Dorman & Co.
Printed and bound in Great Britain by Mackays of Chatham plc, Kent.

Papers used by Ebury Press are natural recyclable products made from wood grown in
sustainable forests.

Contents

Cookery Notes

- All recipes serve 2, unless otherwise indicated.
- Both metric and imperial measures are given for the recipes. Follow one set of measurements only, not a combination, because they are not interchangeable.
- All spoon measures are level unless otherwise stated.
- Ovens must be preheated to the specified temperature. Grills should also be preheated.
- Large eggs should be used except where otherwise specified. Free-range eggs are recommended.
- Use fresh herbs unless otherwise suggested.
- Stocks should be freshly made if possible. Alternatively buy good quality ready-made stock.
- If you do not have an ice-cream maker, freeze ice cream in a shallow container, whisking several times during freezing to ensure an even-textured result.

Foreword

It seems like a contradiction in terms, but quite often the word 'mature' was on the minds of my fellow judges and I as we watched, waited and tasted our way through this series of Junior MasterChef. The ingredients, techniques and final results were almost always surprisingly mature and it has been mentioned by many judges that the cooking on the series could just as easily have been whipped up by the older contestants on MasterChef. One of my concerns since we first started planning Junior MasterChef was the fear that we would have too much artfully precocious cooking that lost many of the young cooks' virtues in an attempt to be grown up. Thankfully that hasn't happened and our junior contestants have consistently put a different spin on their cooking.

Our cooks inventiveness really shone when it came to naming dishes. I will never forget the bewildered curiosity of reading Luke Temple's menu which culminated in a pudding called Mango Meringue Chinchilla with Coconut and Chilli Ice Cream. The chinchilla part of the title remained a mystery. Not so with Isosceles Roast Potatoes: little triangles obviously inspired by Alice Broad's love of geometry. Potatoes by the way were big news in Junior Masterchef this year with our contestants dishing up a staggering number of different ways to cook them, ranging from classics like Dauphinoise Potatoes to the less well known Potato and Parsnip Rösti, or Sliced Potatoes baked with Tomato and Basil.

Ironically, in a year in which concern over children's eating habits promoted food manufacturers to concoct the absurdity of chocolate flavoured vegetables, our juniors were cooking more healthily than ever before. Vegetables were consistently cooked with great care and attention and puddings featured fruit far more often than chocolate.

Of course the menus of Junior MasterChef reflect an awareness of trends in the food world and in our 1998 menus fish was in front of other main course ingredients. Our contestants chose a good variety of fish too. Yes we had salmon and cod, but also sea bass, skate, turbot and swordfish. Beef only cropped up on one menu, but lamb was consistently popular and pork was a feature of five menus. I am still concerned that we attract so few vegetarian cooks and would also like to see more menus featuring Indian or Afro-Caribbean dishes. Additional good news this year was the diligence with which many of our cooks sought out great British ingredients. Whilst I welcome all the exotic ingredients and techniques that are a hallmark of modern cooking, I would like to emphasise that the bedrock of cooking has to be carefully chosen seasonal, local ingredients.

Finally two notable and unusual firsts amongst our competitors this year. Claire and Sara Kent were the first siblings to compete against each other, and Courtney Lewis cooked with a broken leg. Who knows what innovations – gastronomic or otherwise – next year might bring.

Once again I am grateful to the families and friends of our young cooks who come along to lend moral support. While the cooks are in the red, yellow and blue kitchens their supporters watch the competition from the green room which I can promise you is filled with just as much drama, stress and excitement. Maybe someday I'll share some tales from the green room with you. But until then, "Let's get cooking!"

Loyd Grossman

Introduction

As you watch and marvel at the twenty-seven ten to fifteen-year-olds who cook their hearts out during the series, you may find yourself wondering about the path which has led them to the red, yellow and blue kitchens.

It all starts with an application form, accompanied by the competition rules. You are asked to tell us a little about yourself, and describe what you would like to cook for us if you are chosen to take part in our regional 'cook-offs'. These are held in catering colleges throughout Britain, and the best sixteen applicants are invited to come and cook for three hungry judges – and happily I am often one of these, along with a top chef and a college lecturer.

We taste eight meals in the morning, another eight in the afternoon, and our 'nibbling, quibbling and ruminating' results in four young cooks being chosen – three to represent the region on television and one reserve.

Next come the short biography pieces which introduce you as you sit on the big breadboard. Our researcher visits you at home and finds out all about your family, your hobbies, what you enjoy at school. Then our small camera crew arrives for about half a day to film you in action.

After this you have a few weeks for some serious practice before we invite you and members of your family to come to the studio for the competition itself. The rest you know!

If you would like to have a go, we promise you that the whole competition will be great fun. Just send a large stamped self-addressed envelope to:

Junior MasterChef
Department BK, PO Box 359
Norwich, Norfolk NR10 4UU

Meanwhile we hope you enjoy this series, don't guess all the winners, and have a great time cooking the scrumptious recipes in this book.

Richard Bryan
Producer & Director
MasterChef

Fish
& Shellfish

Poached Fillet of Salmon with a Lime and Ginger Sauce

2 salmon fillets, each about 125 g (4 oz)
grated zest and juice of 1 lime, or to taste
300 ml (½ pint) fish stock
15 g (½ oz) fresh root ginger, peeled and
   finely chopped
2.5 ml (½ tsp) beurre manié (see note)
30-45 ml (2-3 tbsp) double cream

To Serve:
Layered Vegetables (see page 59)
Almond Potatoes (see page 76)

1 Place the salmon fillets in an oval ovenproof dish. Sprinkle with lime zest and a little lime juice.

2 Bring the stock to the boil in a saucepan, then pour around the salmon fillets. Add the chopped ginger, then cover the dish with buttered foil.

3 Bake in a preheated oven at 180°C (350°F) mark 4 for 10-15 minutes until the fish is just cooked.

4 Strain off some of the stock from the dish into a small pan; keep the salmon warm in a low oven. Boil the stock rapidly to reduce by half. Check the seasoning. Whisk in the beurre manié over the heat to thicken the sauce. Just before serving, stir in the cream.

5 Transfer the salmon fillets to warmed serving plates and pour on the sauce. Serve at once, with the layered vegetables and almond potatoes.

Note: For the beurre manié, knead together equal quantities of softened butter and flour.

Salmon Fillets with a Sun-dried Tomato, Basil and Cream Sauce

2 salmon fillets, each 175 g (6 oz)
25-50 g (1-2 oz) butter

Sauce:
125 ml (4 fl oz) Noilly Prat
250 ml (8 fl oz) double cream
6 basil leaves, chopped
15 g (½ oz) sun-dried tomatoes, chopped
squeeze of lemon juice, to taste
salt and freshly ground black pepper

To Serve:
Stir-fried Sugar Snap Peas and Cucumber
* (see page 54)*
new potatoes

1 First prepare the sauce. Pour the Noilly Prat into a saucepan, bring to the boil and reduce by half. Leave to cool.

2 Put the cream in another saucepan and boil to reduce by about one third, until thick and golden. Add the chopped basil leaves and sun-dried tomatoes, and the reduced Noilly Prat. Sharpen to taste with lemon juice and season with salt and pepper.

3 Place the salmon fillets on a baking sheet and top each with a large knob of butter, but no seasoning. Bake in a preheated oven at 200°C (400°F) mark 6 for 5 minutes only.

4 To serve, transfer the salmon fillets to warmed serving plates. Pour the sauce to one side of the fish and serve at once, accompanied by the stir-fried vegetables and new potatoes.

Marinated Seared Thai Salmon in a Ginger and Teryaki Sauce with a Sweet Ginger Relish

350 g (12 oz) salmon fillet, with skin

Marinade:
7.5 ml (1½ tsp) caster sugar
2 ml (⅓ tsp) grated fresh root ginger
30 ml (2 tbsp) kukoman soy sauce
15 ml (1 tbsp) mirin
15 ml (1 tbsp) saké

Sweet Ginger Relish:
50 g (2 oz) fresh root ginger (see note)
15 ml (1 tbsp) sugar
60 ml (4 tbsp) rice wine vinegar
1.25 ml (¼ tsp) salt

To Serve:
Caramelised Roasted Garlic Spinach (see page 63)
Japanese Rice (see page 82)

1 Mix together the ingredients for the marinade in a shallow dish. Lay the fish in the dish, skin-side up, cover and leave to marinate in the refrigerator overnight if possible, or for several hours.

2 To prepare the relish, peel the ginger and cut into wafer-thin slices, using a swivel vegetable peeler or mandolin. Place in a saucepan and add boiling water to cover. Simmer for 15-20 minutes, then drain and place in a bowl. Mix together the sugar, vinegar and salt, then pour over the cooked ginger and leave to stand for at least 30 minutes.

3 To cook the salmon, preheat the grill to high. Lay the fish on the grill rack, flesh-side up, and baste with the soy and ginger marinade. Grill for 2-3 minutes, then carefully turn the fish over and grill for a further 4-5 minutes until the skin is caramelised and 'puffed up'.

4 Cut the salmon into two portions and place on warmed serving plates. Spoon over the cooking juices and serve at once, with the sweet ginger relish, spinach and Japanese rice.

Salmon in a White Wine, Cucumber and Dill Sauce

2 salmon fillets
60 g (2¼ oz) butter

Sauce:
½ cucumber
275 ml (9 fl oz) fish stock (see below)
275 ml (9 fl oz) white wine
15 ml (1 tbsp) finely chopped dill
15 ml (1 tbsp) double cream
knob of butter (optional)

To Serve:
Champ (see page 72)
roasted baby plum tomatoes (see below)

1 For the sauce, peel the cucumber, halve lengthwise and scoop out the seeds. Chop the cucumber flesh finely and place in a saucepan with the stock and wine. Heat until the cucumber is transparent, then add the chopped dill.

2 Meanwhile, cook the salmon. Heat the butter in a heavy-based frying pan; allow it to brown very slightly, but make sure it doesn't burn. Add the salmon fillets and fry for about 1½ minutes on each side, until golden brown on the outside, but still barely cooked in the middle.

3 Stir the cream into the sauce, and add a knob of butter it it seems too thick.

4 To serve, transfer the salmon to warmed plates and surround with the sauce. Serve with the champ and roasted tomatoes.

Fish Stock: Put 1.5 kg (3½ lb) fish heads and bones in a large saucepan and add plenty of water to cover. Bring to the boil, lower the heat and simmer for 20 minutes. Take out the fish heads and bones, then strain the stock through a fine sieve, or muslin. Return the stock to the pan. Add 1 onion, chopped; 1 leek, chopped; a handful of mushrooms; 1 large carrot, chopped; 1 celery stick, chopped. Simmer for 45 minutes, then strain to remove the vegetables. Use as required.

Roasted Baby Plum Tomatoes: Immerse the tomatoes in boiling water for about 30 seconds, then remove and peel away the skins. Put the skinned tomatoes into a baking dish, sprinkle with chopped garlic and roast in a preheated oven at 220°C (425°F) mark 7 for 20 minutes or until caramelised.

Peppered Swordfish on a bed of Camargue Rice with a Thai Sauce and Sweet Potato Crisps

2 swordfish steaks, each about 175 g (6 oz)
olive oil, for brushing
few black peppercorns
salt and freshly ground black pepper

Marinade:
juice of 1 lime
15 ml (1 tbsp) Thai fish sauce
15 ml (1 tbsp) olive oil

Rice:
150 g (5 oz) red Camargue rice
few drops of olive oil
1 shallot, finely chopped
15 ml (1 tbsp) pine nuts

Thai Sauce:
2 shallots, chopped
1 lemon grass stalk, chopped
1 small green chilli, seeded and chopped
1 small piece fresh root ginger, peeled and
   chopped
1 clove garlic, chopped
few drops of olive oil
300 ml (½ pint) fish stock
200 ml (7 fl oz) coconut milk
100 ml (3½ fl oz) crème fraîche
large bunch of coriander, stalks removed,
   chopped

Sweet Potato Crisps:
1 long sweet potato
oil, for deep-frying

To Serve:
coriander sprigs, to garnish
Lamb's Leaf Salad with a Raspberry
   Vinaigrette (see page 54)

1   Combine the marinade ingredients in a shallow dish. Add the swordfish steaks and turn to coat in the mixture. Cover and leave to marinate in a cool place for 1 hour.

2   Cook the rice in boiling salted water, according to packet instructions, for about 30 minutes until *al dente*, tender but firm to the bite. Heat a few drops of oil in a frying pan, add the shallot and fry gently until softened. Add the pine nuts and fry until lightly coloured; set aside.

3   In the meantime, prepare the sauce. Put the shallots, lemon grass, chilli, ginger and garlic in a frying pan with a few drops of olive oil and fry gently until softened. Add the fish stock and let bubble until reduced by half. Pass through a sieve and return to the frying pan. Stir in the coconut, crème fraîche and seasoning to taste; keep warm.

4   To cook the fish, preheat a griddle or heavy-based frying pan until very hot and lightly brush with olive oil. Lift the fish steaks out of the marinade, crush some peppercorns on top of them and place on the griddle. Fry for 3 minutes each side, or until just cooked through.

5   Meanwhile, prepare the crisps. Peel the sweet potato and pare into long thin strips, using a swivel potato peeler. Heat the oil for deep-frying in a suitable pan until very hot. Add the sweet potato slices and deep-fry for 2 minutes or until crisp and golden brown. Drain on kitchen paper and season with a little salt.

6   Stir the chopped coriander into the Thai sauce. Drain the rice as soon as it is cooked and toss with the fried shallot and pine nuts. Spoon a bed of rice onto each warmed serving plate and place a swordfish steak on top. Pour on the sauce and garnish with coriander sprigs. Serve with the sweet potato crisps and salad.

Pan-fried Swordfish Steak on a bed of Marinated Aubergine

For this recipe, the marinated aubergine needs to be prepared a day ahead.

2 swordfish steaks
30 ml (2 tbsp) olive oil

Marinated Aubergine:
1 aubergine
salt and freshly ground black pepper
50 ml (2 fl oz) olive oil
10 ml (2 tsp) thin honey
45 ml (3 tbsp) white wine vinegar
8 basil leaves, roughly torn

Lemon Dressing:
15 ml (1 tbsp) lemon juice
30 ml (2 tbsp) olive oil
1 clove garlic, crushed
2.5 ml (½ tsp) dry mustard
5 ml (1 tsp) chopped parsley

Tomato Concassé:
1 tomato, skinned, seeded and diced

To Serve:
sautéed potatoes, flavoured with saffron

1 To prepare the aubergine, cut into slices, sprinkle with salt and leave to degorge for about 30 minutes. Rinse to remove excess salt, drain and pat dry with kitchen paper.

2 Heat the olive oil in a large heavy-based frying pan and fry the aubergine slices gently until soft. Season with salt and pepper. Transfer the aubergines to a shallow dish and drizzle over the honey and vinegar. Scatter the basil leaves on top. Cover with cling film and refrigerate overnight.

3 The following day, lay the aubergines in an ovenproof dish and reheat in a preheated oven at 180°C (350°F) mark 4 for 5 minutes.

4 In the meantime, cook the fish. Heat the oil in a heavy-based frying pan and fry the swordfish for 3 minutes each side or until cooked. Season with salt and pepper.

5 Meanwhile, whisk the lemon dressing ingredients together in a bowl until evenly amalgamated; season with salt and pepper to taste. Warm through in a small pan (or in the microwave).

6 Arrange a bed of aubergine slices on each warmed serving plate and place the swordfish steaks on top. Sprinkle with the tomato concassé and surround with the warm lemon dressing. Serve immediately, with sautéed potatoes.

Pan-fried Turbot on a bed of Caramelised Shallots with a Beurre Blanc Sauce

2 medium turbot fillets
salt and freshly ground black pepper
juice of ½ lemon
25 g (1 oz) butter
10 ml (2 tsp) olive oil

Caramelised Shallots:
10 shallots
25 g (1 oz) butter
100 ml (3½ fl oz) water
50 ml (2 fl oz) white wine
50 g (2 oz) brown sugar

Beurre Blanc:
75 ml (5 tbsp) fish stock
50 ml (2 fl oz) white wine
salt and freshly ground white pepper
75 g (3 oz) unsalted butter, diced

To Serve:
turned vegetables (eg carrots and courgettes)

1 Trim the turbot fillets, season with salt and pepper and squeeze over the lemon juice. Cover and place in the refrigerator while preparing the shallots.

2 Peel and thinly slice the shallots. Melt the butter in a small heavy-based pan, add the shallots and fry for 2 minutes.

3 Add the water and let bubble to reduce by two thirds. Season with salt and pepper to taste. Add the wine and brown sugar and cook, stirring frequently, for about 10 minutes until the shallots have caramelised.

4 In the meantime, prepare the beurre blanc. Bring the fish stock to the boil in a small saucepan and add the wine and seasoning. Let bubble to reduce by half. Just before serving, whisk in the butter, a piece at a time.

5 Meanwhile, cook the turbot. Heat the butter and oil in a heavy-based frying pan. Add the turbot fillets and fry for about 2½ minutes on each side; do not overcook.

6 To serve, put the caramelised shallots in the middle of the warmed serving plates and top with the turbot fillets. Surround with the beurre blanc sauce and serve at once, accompanied by the vegetables.

Note: To 'turn' vegetables, simply chisel into batons of uniform size and shape before cooking. Courgettes and carrots are suitable.

Sea Bass with a Basil and Pine Nut Crust, served with a Parsley Sauce

2 sea bass fillets, each about 125 g (4 oz)
25 g (1 oz) butter
1 shallot, chopped
1 clove garlic, finely chopped
300 ml (½ pint) court bouillon (see below)

Basil and Pine Nut Crust:
25 g (1 oz) pine nuts, toasted
15 ml (1 tbsp) olive oil
25 g (1 oz) fresh white breadcrumbs
10 basil leaves, finely chopped
sea salt and freshly ground black pepper

Sauce:
25 g (1 oz) butter, diced
small bunch of flat-leaf parsley, stalks
 removed, roughly chopped
juice of ¼ lemon

To Serve:
griddled (or roasted) cherry tomatoes

1 Trim the sea bass fillets, if required, and remove any residual bones with tweezers.

2 To make the basil and pine nut crust, put the pine nuts into a blender with the olive oil and work to a rough paste. Mix the breadcrumbs and basil together in a bowl, then add the pine nut paste and mix well. Season with salt and pepper to taste.

3 To cook the fish, heat the butter in a frying pan, add the shallot and garlic and fry gently until softened. Pour in the court bouillon, then add the sea bass fillets and poach gently for 5 minutes. Remove the fish fillets with a fish slice; they should still be slightly undercooked. Strain and reserve the cooking liquor.

4 Spoon the crust on top of the fish fillets and press firmly to adhere. Place in a flameproof dish and cook under a preheated grill for about 1 minute, until the crust is golden brown and crisp.

5 Meanwhile, to make the sauce, pour the cooking liquor into a saucepan, bring to the boil and whisk in the butter, parsley and lemon juice.

6 To serve, transfer the fish to warmed serving plates and arrange the tomatoes alongside. Pour some of the sauce around the fish and serve immediately.

Note: To make the court bouillon, pour 900 ml (1½ pints) water into a saucepan, add 1 carrot, quartered; 1 onion, quartered; a bouquet garni; 6 black peppercorns and 250 ml (8 fl oz) dry white wine. Bring to the boil and simmer, uncovered, for about 30 minutes. Strain and use as required.

Tranche of Cod Viennoise, served with a Thai Seafood Sauce

8 button mushrooms, finely sliced
5 ml (1 tsp) olive oil
150 ml (¼ pint) whipping cream
3 tomatoes
1 clove garlic, crushed
½ small onion, finely chopped
4 slices white bread, crusts removed
50 g (2 oz) Gruyère cheese, grated
75 g (3 oz) unsalted butter, melted
1-2 parsley sprigs
salt and freshly ground black pepper
2 cod fillets, each about 175 g (6 oz)
30 ml (2 tbsp) Dijon mustard
30 ml (2 tbsp) white wine
30 ml (2 tbsp) olive oil
squeeze of lemon juice

Sauce:
150 ml (¼ pint) whipping cream
20 ml (4 tsp) white wine
15 ml (1 tbsp) oyster sauce
15 ml (1 tbsp) Thai fish sauce
2 pinches of saffron threads
15 ml (1 tbsp) finely chopped parsley

To Serve:
spinach
new potatoes

1 Put the diced mushrooms in a small pan with the olive oil. Cover and sweat for about 3 minutes. Add the cream, bring to the boil and let bubble until thickened to a paste-like consistency.

2 Immerse the tomatoes in boiling water for 1 minute, then remove and peel away the skins. Halve the tomatoes, deseed and roughly chop the flesh. Place in a pan with the garlic, onion and a drop of olive oil. Cover and sweat gently until the tomatoes are soft.

3 Break up the bread, put into the food processor and process to crumbs. Add the cheese, melted butter and parsley sprig(s). Process until evenly blended; do not over-mix or the mixture will be too soft. Season with salt and pepper.

4 Season the cod fillets with salt and pepper. Spread 15 ml (1 tbsp) of Dijon mustard on top of each fish fillet, then cover with the tomato mixture. Next spread on the mushroom paste. Finally, cover with the soft herb crust. (The easiest way to apply the crust is to roughly form it into the shape of the cod fillet with your hands before placing it on the fish.)

5 Transfer the cod fillets to an ovenproof dish and add the white wine, olive oil and lemon juice. Bake in a preheated oven at 190°C (375°F) mark 5 for 20-22 minutes.

6 Meanwhile, make the sauce. Bring the cream to the boil in a heavy-based pan, then add all the other sauce ingredients. Bring back to the boil and let bubble for 1 minute, stirring all the time, to reduce slightly.

7 Once the fish is cooked, remove from the dish and place under a preheated high grill for 30 seconds until the herb crust is golden brown.

8 Serve the cod fillets on a bed of spinach, surrounded by the sauce and accompanied by new potatoes.

Skate Fillet stuffed with Air-dried Ham, served with a Red Pepper Sauce

2 skate fillets
4 strips of Parma ham
plain flour, for coating
salt and freshly ground black pepper
25 ml (5 tsp) olive oil

Red Pepper Sauce:
2 shallots, peeled
1 carrot, peeled
1 red pepper, halved, cored and seeded
30 ml (2 tbsp) olive oil
30 ml (2 tbsp) tomato paste
50 g (2 oz) butter
1 bay leaf
1 thyme sprig
200 ml (7 fl oz) fish stock
100 ml (3½ fl oz) white wine
12 capers

To Serve:
Citrus Leeks with Sugar Snap Peas (see page 61)
Timbale of Mixed Rice (see page 83)

1 First make the red pepper sauce. Cut the shallots, carrot and red pepper into cubes. Heat the olive oil in a heavy-based saucepan, add the cubed vegetables, cover and sweat over a medium heat for approximately 5 minutes.

2 Meanwhile, cut each skate fillet in half. Lay the Parma ham strips on two of the skate pieces and sandwich together in pairs with the other pieces of fish. Coat evenly with flour and season with pepper and a little salt.

3 Add the tomato paste to the red pepper sauce with the butter, bay leaf and thyme. Reduce the heat slightly and cook gently for 2-4 minutes.

4 To cook the fish, heat the oil in a heavy-based frying pan until very hot. Add the skate sandwiches and fry for approximately 30 seconds on each side. Transfer to a shallow baking tin and cook in a preheated oven at 200°C (400°F) mark 6 for about 10 minutes until the fish is cooked through.

5 Meanwhile, add the fish stock, wine and capers to the sauce and stir well.

6 To serve, transfer the fish to warmed serving plates and pour on the sauce. Serve immediately, with the vegetables and rice.

Smoked Haddock with a Lemon and Cream Sauce

2 fillets undyed smoked haddock, each about
  150 g (5 oz)
light fish stock or water, for poaching
1 bay leaf
few peppercorns

Sauce:
20 g (¾ oz) butter
20 g (¾ oz) plain flour
300 ml (½ pint) fish stock
30 ml (2 tbsp) whipping cream
15 ml (1 tbsp) lemon juice
salt and freshly ground black pepper

To Serve:
steamed Savoy cabbage leaves, to garnish
Colcannon (see page 67)

1 To make the sauce, melt the butter in a saucepan, stir in the flour and cook, stirring, for 1 minute. Gradually stir in the fish stock. Bring to the boil, stirring constantly, and cook for 2-3 minutes until thickened and smooth. Stir in the cream and lemon juice. Season with salt and pepper to taste. Keep warm.

2 To cook the fish, gently poach the smoked haddock in a little fish stock or water, with the bay leaf and peppercorns added, for 7-10 minutes until just opaque and tender.

3 To serve, carefully drain the smoked haddock fillets and place on warmed serving plates. Pour on the lemon sauce and serve, garnished with cabbage leaves and accompanied by the colcannon.

Medley of Seafood on a bed of Spinach with Deep-fried Carrot Julienne, Steamed Potatoes and a Tarragon Dressing

If possible, prepare the dressing a day in advance to allow time for the flavours to infuse.

Dressing:
30 ml (2 tbsp) olive oil
5 ml (1 tsp) balsamic vinegar
5 ml (1 tsp) wholegrain mustard
15 ml (1 tbsp) clarified butter
1 tarragon sprig
salt and freshly ground black pepper

Seafood Medley:
1 salmon fillet, about 100 g (4 oz) and
2 cm (¾ inch) thick
1 coley fillet, about 100 g (4 oz) and 2 cm
(¾ inch) thick
1 pollack fillet, about 100 g (4 oz) and
2 cm (¾ inch) thick
30 ml (2 tbsp) olive oil
25 g (1 oz) butter
1 tarragon sprig, chopped

Vegetables:
8 small potatoes
3 large carrots, peeled
seasoned flour, for coating
oil, for deep-frying
100 g (4 oz) spinach leaves, trimmed

To Garnish:
few cooked shellfish (eg prawns and mussels
in shells)
tarragon sprigs

1 To make the dressing, whizz the ingredients in a blender until amalgamated and the tarragon is finely chopped.

2 Cut each fish fillet into two equal-sized pieces, removing any residual bones with tweezers. Set aside.

3 Peel the potatoes and cut into even-sized slices.

4 Cut the carrots into long fine julienne, or matchstick strips. Dry on kitchen paper, then shake in seasoned flour. Heat the oil for frying in a deep-fat fryer.

5 Meanwhile, start to cook the fish. Heat the oil, butter and chopped tarragon in a heavy-based frying pan. Add the fish and fry for about 3 minutes each side until opaque.

6 While the fish is cooking, put the potato slices in a microwave steamer with 30 ml (2 tbsp) water and cook on HIGH for 3 minutes (see note). Drain.

7 Shake excess flour off the carrots and deep-fry in the hot oil for 2-3 minutes or until crispy. Drain on kitchen paper.

8 Steam the spinach for 3-5 minutes or cook in a tightly covered pan with just the water clinging to the leaves after washing, until just wilted. Drain thoroughly.

9 Warm the shellfish and dressing.

10 To serve, place a large mound of crispy carrots in the centre of each warmed serving plate. Surround with 3 spoonfuls of spinach and place one piece of each fish on each mound of spinach. Place slices of potato between the fish. Pour the dressing over the fish and garnish with the shellfish and tarragon. Serve at once.

Note: Alternatively, cook the potato conventionally in boiling salted water, but start cooking earlier, at stage 3.

Seafood Roulade with a Lime and Watercress Hollandaise

*2 strips of tail end salmon fillet, each 20 cm
  (8 inches) long and 2.5 cm (1 inch) wide*
*2 strips of lemon sole fillet, each 20 cm
  (8 inches) long and 2.5 cm (1 inch) wide*
2 scallops, shelled and cleaned
squeeze of lime juice
15 ml (1 tbsp) olive oil
salt and freshly ground black pepper
knob of butter

Hollandaise:
2 egg yolks
pinch of salt
10 ml (2 tsp) finely grated lime zest
10 ml (2 tsp) lime juice
10 ml (2 tsp) white wine vinegar
100 g (4 oz) salted butter, melted
*handful of watercress, stalks removed,
  chopped*

To Serve:
*Rice Noodles with Shiitake Mushrooms and
  Oyster Sauce (see page 82)*
*Stir-fried vegetables (eg sliced carrots, green
  beans, sweetcorn and asparagus)*

1 Trim the fish fillets as necessary and remove any residual bones with tweezers.

2 Wrap each piece of salmon around a scallop, then wrap the lemon sole fillet around the salmon. Secure with wooden cocktail sticks or short kebab skewers. Place in a shallow dish, sprinkle with the lime juice, a little olive oil and seasoning. Leave to marinate in a cool place until ready to cook.

3 To make the hollandaise, put the egg yolks and salt in a food processor or blender and process briefly. Heat the lime zest, lime juice and vinegar together in a small pan. With the motor running, slowly pour the hot lime mixture through the feeder tube onto the egg yolks, then add the melted butter in a thin steady stream. The mixture should be thick and pale. Finally, add the watercress and process briefly until evenly blended.

4 To cook the fish, heat the butter and 7.5 ml (½ tbsp) olive oil in a small frying pan. Add the seafood roulades and fry gently for 6 minutes each side.

5 Transfer the seafood roulades to warmed serving plates and pour on a little of the hollandaise sauce. Serve accompanied by the rice noodles, stir-fried vegetables and remaining hollandaise.

Poultry
& Game

Chicken Breast stuffed with Peppers

2 skinless chicken breast fillets
salt and freshly ground black pepper
olive oil, for brushing
5 ml (1 tsp) chopped mixed herbs (eg parsley,
 oregano, basil)
30 ml (2 tbsp) single cream

Stuffing:
½ red pepper, seeded
½ green pepper, seeded
½ yellow pepper, seeded
½ onion
2 mushrooms
1 clove garlic
15 ml (1 tbsp) olive oil
15 ml (1 tbsp) brown sugar
15 ml (1 tbsp) red wine vinegar
15 ml (1 tbsp) sherry
15 ml (1 tbsp) chopped walnuts

To Serve:
Stir-fried Vegetable Bundles (see page 57)
Potato and Parsnip Rösti (see page 68)

1 First prepare the stuffing. Chop all of the vegetables and the garlic by hand or in a food processor. Heat the oil in a small pan, add the chopped vegetables together with the rest of the stuffing ingredients. Bring to a simmer and cook gently for 20 minutes. Allow to cool.

2 Cut a deep horizontal slit in the side of each chicken breast and fill with some of the stuffing mixture. Secure the opening with wooden cocktail sticks. Season the chicken with salt and pepper, brush with oil and sprinkle with the chopped herbs; press down to adhere. Reserve the rest of the pepper mixture.

3 Preheat an ovenproof skillet on the hob and brush with oil. Lay the chicken breasts on the hot skillet and quickly sear on both sides. Transfer to the preheated oven at 180°C (350°F) mark 4 and bake for 20-30 minutes, until tender.

4 Before serving, reheat the reserved pepper mixture and stir in the cream; do not boil. Remove the cocktail sticks from the chicken and place on warmed serving plates. Pour on the sauce and serve with the vegetable accompaniments.

Grilled Turmeric Chicken, served with a Watercress Sauce

For this dish, the chicken needs to be marinated a day in advance.

2 skinless chicken breast fillets

Marinade:
100 g (3½ oz) Greek-style yogurt
5 ml (1 tsp) turmeric
1 cm (½ inch) piece fresh root ginger, peeled and grated
½ clove garlic, crushed

Sauce:
30 g (1 oz) watercress sprigs, stalks removed
30 ml (2 tbsp) double cream
30 g (1 oz) butter, diced
2.5 ml (½ tsp) lemon juice
salt and freshly ground black pepper

To Serve:
Basil-fried Potato Balls (see page 73)
Garlic Acorn-squash (see page 66)

1 For the marinade, mix the yogurt, turmeric, ginger and garlic together in a shallow dish. Add the chicken breasts and turn to coat in the yogurt mixture. Cover the dish and leave to marinate in the refrigerator for 24 hours.

2 The next day, blanch the watercress sprigs in boiling water for 2 minutes. Drain, reserving 30 ml (2 tbsp) of the water; let cool.

3 Cook the chicken under a preheated hot grill for 20 minutes, turning once and basting with the marinade from time to time.

4 Meanwhile, make the sauce. Place the reserved watercress water in a pan with the cream. Bring to the boil and whisk in the butter. Add the watercress and lemon juice. Season with salt and pepper to taste.

5 Transfer the grilled chicken to warmed serving plates and pour on the watercress sauce. Serve at once, with the potato balls and acorn squash.

Breast of Chicken stuffed with Wild Mushroom Forcemeat, served with Pan-fried Chicken Livers

2 chicken breast fillets
75 g (3 oz) sausagemeat
2 chanterelles or shiitake mushrooms, chopped
½ shallot, finely chopped
5 ml (1 tsp) shelled pistachio nuts
salt and freshly ground black pepper
30 ml (2 tbsp) oil
1 large potato, peeled and cut into cubes
pinch of saffron strands
60 ml (4 tbsp) white wine
60 ml (4 tbsp) double cream
15 g (½ oz) butter
5 cm (2 inch) piece fresh root ginger, peeled and shredded
1 leek, trimmed and cut into julienne strips
1 carrot, peeled and cut into julienne strips
125 g (4 oz) chicken livers, trimmed
100 g (4 oz) thin honey
5 ml (1 tsp) caraway seeds
5 ml (1 tsp) ground cumin
30 ml (2 tbsp) liquid glucose

To Serve:
saffron potatoes
julienne of vegetables

1 Make a deep slit in the side of each chicken breast fillet to form a pocket.

2 In a bowl, mix the sausagemeat with the mushrooms, shallot, pistachio nuts and seasoning until evenly combined. Press the forcemeat into the chicken breast pockets, spreading it evenly.

3 Heat the oil in a heavy-based frying pan, add the chicken breast fillets and quickly brown on each side. Transfer to a baking tin and cook in a preheated oven at 200°C (400°F) mark 6 for 20 minutes.

4 Meanwhile, put the potato in a small pan with just enough water to cover and the saffron. Cook until tender, then add the wine and reduce down. Transfer the potato to a warmed dish, cover and keep warm. Add the cream to the pan and reduce to a good sauce consistency.

5 Melt the butter in another pan. Add the ginger, leek, carrot and seasoning and stir-fry over a high heat for 2 minutes; keep hot.

6 Heat the oil remaining in the frying pan (the chicken was sealed in). Add the chicken livers and fry quickly until browned. Transfer to a small baking tin and cook in the oven for 4 minutes.

7 Meanwhile, put the honey, caraway and cumin in a small pan and heat through. Stir in the glucose.

8 To serve, slice each stuffed chicken breast into 3 pieces and arrange on the warmed serving plates. Place the chicken livers on the plates and pile the vegetable julienne on top. Add the saffron potatoes and pour the honey sauce and cream sauce around the edge of the plates.

Chicken Breast filled with Courgette and Pistachio Nut Stuffing, served with Red Pepper Sauce

2 skinless chicken breast fillets

Stuffing:

1 slice white bread, crusts removed
15 g (½ oz) onion, finely chopped
25 g (1 oz) soft cheese with garlic and herbs
  (eg Boursin)
25 g (1 oz) courgette, grated
7.5 ml (1½ tsp) chopped parsley
15 g (½ oz) pistachio nuts, roughly chopped
salt and freshly ground black pepper

Red Pepper Sauce:

1 red pepper, halved, cored, seeded and
  roughly chopped
15 g (½ oz) unsalted butter
90 ml (6 tbsp) chicken stock
5 ml (1 tsp) sugar
5 ml (1 tsp) tomato paste
30 ml (2 tbsp) single cream

To Serve:

split pistachio nuts, to garnish
Individual Dauphinoise Potatoes
  (see page 80)
stir-fried green vegetables

1 Remove the sinew from the back of each chicken breast, then fold back the fillet so that it opens out like a book. Place each fillet between two sheets of grease-proof paper and flatten with a rolling pin until slightly longer and thinner.

2 For the stuffing, break up the bread and work in a food processor or blender to fine crumbs. Place in a bowl with the onion, cheese, grated courgette, parsley and pistachio nuts. Mix well and season generously with salt and pepper.

3 Divide the stuffing between the flattened chicken breast fillets, and spread evenly, then roll up tightly. Wrap each one in a piece of buttered foil and chill in the refrigerator for 20 minutes.

4 Put the foil-wrapped chicken breasts in a roasting tin and bake in a preheated oven at 220°C (425°F) mark 7 for 20 minutes.

5 Meanwhile, make the red pepper sauce. Put the red pepper in a heavy based pan with the butter, cover and sweat over a low heat for 10-15 minutes. Purée the softened pepper with the stock, sugar and tomato paste in a blender (or using a hand-held blender). Pass through a sieve and return to the pan. Stir in the cream and season with salt and pepper to taste; keep warm.

6 After baking, leave the chicken to rest in a warm place for 10 minutes. To serve, unwrap and slice thickly on the diagonal into neat slices. Arrange on individual serving plates and pour on the red pepper sauce. Scatter over the split pistachio nuts to garnish. Serve with the dauphinoise potatoes and stir-fried green vegetables.

Note: If you prefer the appearance of the red pepper shreds in the sauce, do not pass through the sieve.

Sautéed Chicken stuffed with Pine Nuts and Apricots on a bed of Stir-fried Leek and Bacon

2½ skinless chicken breasts
15 ml (1 tbsp) olive oil

Stuffing:
1 egg yolk
5 ml (1 tsp) olive oil
100 g (4 oz) no-need-to-soak dried apricots,
  roughly chopped
100 g (4 oz) pine nuts, toasted
salt and freshly ground black pepper

Lemon Sauce:
50 g (2 oz) sugar
300 ml (½ pint) homemade chicken stock
juice of 1 lemon

Stir-fry:
1 leek, trimmed and cut into julienne strips
50 g (2 oz) bacon, derinded and cut into
  julienne strips
dash of sesame oil
sprinkling of sesame seeds

To Serve:
baby carrots
roast parsnips
Parisian potatoes
fine green beans

1 Beat the chicken breasts between two sheets of greaseproof paper, using a rolling pin, to a 5 mm (¼ inch) thickness.

2 To make the stuffing, put the other half chicken breast fillet in a blender with the egg yolk and purée until smooth. Transfer to a bowl and add the 5 ml (1 tsp) olive oil, dried apricots and toasted pine nuts. Mix well and season with salt and pepper to taste.

3 Cut a deep horizontal pocket through the side of each chicken breast and spoon in the stuffing. Secure the opening with wooden cocktail sticks or short wooden kebab skewers.

4 Heat the 15 ml (1 tbsp) olive oil in a heavy-based frying pan, add the stuffed chicken breasts and seal over a moderate heat until golden brown on both sides. Transfer the chicken breasts to a small roasting tin and bake in a preheated oven at 180°C (350°F) mark 4 for 15 minutes, or until cooked through.

5 Meanwhile, make the sauce. Put the sugar in a small heavy-based pan and place over a low heat until melted. Increase the heat to moderate and cook to a golden brown caramel. Carefully add the stock and lemon juice and bring to the boil, stirring.

6 In the meantime, prepare the stir-fried leek and bacon. Heat a little sesame oil in a wok, then add the leek and bacon julienne with a sprinkling of sesame seeds. Stir-fry until the leek is softened and golden, and the bacon is firm.

7 To serve, carve the stuffed chicken breasts into thick slices. Spoon the bacon and leek stir-fry onto warmed serving plates and arrange the chicken on top. Pour on the sauce and serve at once, with the vegetable accompaniments.

Chicken Risotto with Mushrooms and Tomato

30 ml (2 tbsp) oil
2 chicken breast fillets
25 g (1 oz) butter
25 g (1 oz) onion, finely chopped
175 g (6 oz) Arborio rice
600 ml (1 pint) chicken stock
15 g (½ oz) mushrooms, chopped
1 beef tomato, seeded and chopped
flat-leaf parsley, to garnish

1 Heat 30 ml (2 tsp) oil in a frying pan, add the chicken breast fillets and fry for 2-3 minutes, until lightly coloured on both sides. Transfer to a roasting tin and cook in a preheated oven at 180°C (350°F) mark 4 for 20-30 minutes, until tender.

2 Melt the butter in a medium saucepan, add the chopped onion and sweat for 1-2 minutes.

3 Add the rice and stir until the grains are coated in the butter and onion.

4 Gradually add the chicken stock, a ladleful at a time, allowing each addition to be absorbed before adding the next. Continue until the rice is *al dente*, tender but firm to the bite. (You won't need to use all of the stock.)

5 Add the chopped mushrooms and half of the tomato; fork through until evenly mixed.

6 To serve, spoon the risotto onto warmed serving plates. Slice the chicken breasts lengthwise and arrange on top of the risotto. Place small spoonfuls of the remaining tomato around the edge of the plate. Drizzle a little chicken stock around the risotto, garnish with parsley and serve at once.

Barbary Duck with Mango and Damson Sauce

2 barbary duck breasts
salt and freshly ground black pepper
1 medium, ripe mango
30 ml (2 tbsp) damson jam
30 ml (2 tbsp) wine vinegar
2.5 ml (½ tsp) ground allspice

To Serve:
Crunchy-topped Leeks (see page 62)
glazed carrots
Scalloped Potatoes (see page 75)

1 Pat the duck breasts dry with kitchen paper. Place in a small roasting tin, skin-side up and rub salt into the skin. Cook in a preheated oven at 200°C (400°F) mark 6 for 30 minutes.

2 Meanwhile, peel the skin off the mango and, using a sharp knife, slice lengthwise into 1 cm (½ inch) thick slices either side of the stone. Cut the 8 longest slices in half and set aside. Finely chop the rest of the mango.

3 In a small saucepan, mix together the damson jam, wine vinegar, finely chopped mango and allspice. Bring to a simmer and simmer gently for 5 minutes.

4 When the duck is cooked, transfer to a warmed plate and leave to rest in a warm place for 5-10 minutes. Drain off as much fat from the roasting tin as possible and discard. Add the residual duck juices to the damson mixture in the saucepan. Season with salt and pepper to taste. Rub through a coarse sieve into a pan, then reheat the sauce.

5 Warm the 8 large mango slices in the microwave on HIGH for 1 minute.

6 Carve each duck breast, on the diagonal, into 5 slices. Arrange the slices of duck and mango alternately on warmed serving plates, pour over the sauce and serve, with the vegetable accompaniments.

Crispy Roast Duck Breast with Cranberry and Orange Sauce

2 magret duck breasts
salt and freshly ground black pepper
7.5 ml (½ tbsp) olive oil
10 ml (2 tsp) thin honey

Cranberry and Orange Sauce:
225 g (8 oz) cranberries
50 g (2 oz) granulated sugar
200 ml (7 fl oz) red wine
grated zest and juice of ½ orange
15 ml (1 tbsp) red wine vinegar

To Serve:
Potato and Apple Rösti (see page 67)
glazed carrots
sugar snap peas

1 Score the fat on the duck breasts all the way across at 3 mm (⅛ inch) intervals; do not cut through to the flesh. Season with plenty of salt and a little black pepper.

2 To make the cranberry and orange sauce, place all the ingredients in a heavy-based saucepan and bring to a very gentle simmer. Stir well, then allow to barely simmer, uncovered, for about 1 hour – stirring from time to time, until the mixture is reduced to a concentrated mass of glazed cranberries.

3 Preheat the oil in a roasting tin on the hob. Place the duck breasts skin-side down in the pan. Once the duck breasts are cooking fast, turn the heat right down and cook for 15-20 minutes; the layer of skin will cook down to a crackling.

4 Turn the duck breasts over and finish cooking them in a preheated oven at 200°C (400°F) mark 6 for 6-10 minutes, depending on the thickness of the breasts.

5 Spoon the honey on top of the duck breasts and place under a preheated grill until glazed. Leave to rest in a warm place for 5 minutes.

6 Serve the duck breasts with the cranberry and orange sauce, rösti, glazed carrots and sugar snap peas.

Wild Duck Breast with Blackberry Sauce

knob of butter
¼ onion, roughly chopped
1 bacon rasher, derinded and roughly
  chopped
salt and freshly ground black pepper
2 duck breast fillets, fat removed
225 g (8 oz) blackberries
150 ml (¼ pint) red wine
7.5 ml (1½ tsp) caster sugar

To Serve:
duchesse potatoes
glazed carrots
French beans

1 Melt the butter in a heavy-based frying pan. Add the onion, bacon and seasoning. Fry gently until the onion is softened, then move to the side of the pan.

2 Add the duck breasts to the frying pan and fry over a high heat for 1 minute each side to seal.

3 Add the blackberries, red wine and sugar. Cover the pan with foil and simmer for 8 minutes, mashing the fruit gently occasionally during cooking.

4 Lift the duck breasts out of the pan and wipe clean; transfer to a warmed dish, cover and leave to rest in a warm place for 5 minutes.

5 Meanwhile, pass the sauce through a sieve to get rid of the blackberry pips. Return to the cleaned pan and simmer for 3-4 minutes to reduce and thicken.

6 Carve the duck breasts into slices. Pour the sauce onto the warmed serving plates and arrange the duck slices on top. Serve with duchesse potatoes, glazed carrots and French beans.

Vanilla Roasted Duck with Honey Roast Root Vegetables

1 oven-ready Gressingham duck
salt and freshly ground black pepper
2 vanilla pods, split
2 large carrots
2 large parsnips
6 small new potatoes, halved
5 ml (1 tsp) oil
15 g (½ oz) butter
15 ml (1 tbsp) thin honey
1 ripe peach, halved and stoned
175 ml (6 fl oz) hot game jus (see below)
chervil sprigs, to garnish

1 To prepare the duck, season with salt and pepper and sprinkle with the seeds extracted from the vanilla pods.

2 Peel the carrots and parsnips and cut into batons, discarding the parsnip cores.

3 Par-boil the potatoes in boiling salted water for 10-15 minutes; drain thoroughly.

4 Heat the oil in an ovenproof cast-iron frying pan. Add the duck and cook over a moderately high heat, turning until browned all over. Transfer to a preheated oven at 220°C (425°F) mark 7 and roast for 15 minutes, or until cooked through.

5 Meanwhile, heat the butter in a small pan, add the carrots and parsnips and sauté until lightly browned. Transfer to a small roasting tin, drizzle with the honey and season with salt and pepper. Bake in the oven for 15 minutes or until tender. At the same time, roast the potatoes in another small oiled tin for about 15 minutes.

6 Remove the duck from the pan, wrap in foil and leave to rest in a warm place for 10-15 minutes. Meanwhile, pour off most of the duck fat from the cast-iron frying pan, leaving a little in the pan. Place the peach slices, cut-side down, in the pan and fry over a moderate heat until caramelised.

7 Carve the duck and arrange on warmed serving plates with the peach halves and roasted vegetables. Pour the game jus over the meat and garnish with chervil to serve.

Game Jus: Brown about 500 g (1 lb 2 oz) game bones in a heavy-based pan over a moderate heat. Add 750 ml (1¼ pints) vegetable stock and bring to the boil. Simmer for 1 hour, then strain through a fine sieve and return to the pan. Simmer to reduce by about half until the sauce is shiny. Check the seasoning

Pheasant Breast with Brandy and Cream Sauce

2 boneless hen pheasant breasts
2 slices pancetta
a little oil, for cooking

Sauce:
knob of butter
1 shallot, chopped
175 ml (6 fl oz) pheasant stock
7.5 ml (1½ tsp) crab apple jelly
2.5 ml (½ tsp) balsamic vinegar
salt and freshly ground black pepper
22 ml (1½ tbsp) brandy
25 ml (1 fl oz) double cream

To Serve:
Celeriac and Apple Purée (see page 65)
mixed leaf salad

1 Wrap each pheasant breast in a slice of pancetta.

2 Lightly oil a heavy-based frying pan and preheat. Add the pheasant breasts and seal over a high heat for 2-3 minutes, turning to colour on all sides. Transfer to a baking dish and bake in a preheated oven at 170°C (325°F) mark 3 for 10 minutes.

3 Meanwhile, make the sauce. Heat the butter in a pan, add the shallot and fry gently until softened. Add the stock, crab apple jelly, balsamic vinegar, salt and pepper. Bring to the boil and reduce by about half. Add the brandy and reduce a little further. Add the cream and reduce again, to a good sauce consistency. Check the seasoning and strain through a fine sieve into a warm jug.

4 Carve the pheasant into slices and arrange on warmed serving plates. Serve with the sauce, celeriac and apple purée, and a mixed leaf salad.

Meat Dishes

Poached Fillet of Beef in a Madeira Sauce

25 g (1 oz) butter
15 ml (1 tbsp) olive oil
2 fillet steaks, each about 175 g (6 oz)
1 onion, chopped
1 carrot, chopped
4 mushrooms, chopped
90 ml (3 fl oz) Madeira
1 sage leaf, chopped
large pinch of chopped fresh or dried mixed
   herbs
120 ml (4 fl oz) beef stock
salt and freshly ground black pepper

To Serve:
Potato Gratin (see page 77)
Mixed Pepper Stir-fry (see page 62)

1 Heat the butter and oil in a heavy-based pan. Add the fillet steaks and briefly fry over a high heat, turning to sear on all sides and seal in the juices. Transfer the fillet steaks to a plate, cover and set aside.

2 Add the onion and carrot to the same pan and cook gently until soft. Add the chopped mushrooms and 60 ml (2 fl oz) Madeira. Cover and simmer for 15 minutes, add the sage, chopped mixed herbs, stock, seasoning and remaining Madeira.

3 Return the fillet steaks to the pan and poach over a low heat for approximately 15 minutes.

4 Transfer the steaks to a warmed plate; cover and keep warm. Boil the sauce to reduce to the required consistency. Check the seasoning and pass the sauce through a sieve.

5 Slice the beef and arrange on warmed serving plates. Surround with the sauce and serve with the vegetable accompaniments.

Rack of Lamb with a Wild Berry, Mint and Herb Sauce

*1 French-trimmed rack of lamb (with
  6-7 cutlets)*
15 ml (1 tbsp) oil

Sauce:
100 ml (3½ fl oz) red wine
500 ml (16 fl oz) demi glace (see below)
2-3 mint sprigs
1-2 rosemary sprigs
1-2 thyme sprigs
1 bay leaf
30 ml (2 tbsp) redcurrant jelly
100 ml (3½ fl oz) lamb stock (optional)
salt and freshly ground black pepper
75 g (3 oz) cranberries

To Serve:
mint leaves, to garnish
Dauphinoise Potatoes (see page 79)
Purée of Parsnips (see page 66)

1 Make sure the lamb is well trimmed and that the exposed bones are scraped clean. Heat the oil in a large heavy-based frying pan. When it is very hot, add the lamb and quickly seal on all sides until golden. Transfer the lamb to a roasting tin, cover loosely with foil and cook in a preheated oven at 200°C (400°F) mark 6 for 10-15 minutes; it should still be pink in the centre.

2 Meanwhile, heat the frying pan in which the lamb was seared. Add the red wine, stirring to incorporate any meat juices. Let bubble until reduced by half, then add the demi glace sauce, herbs and redcurrant jelly. Thin down with stock if necessary. Check the seasoning. Strain the sauce through a fine sieve into a clean pan and add the cranberries, reserving a few for garnish. Heat the sauce through gently.

3 Carve the lamb evenly into cutlets and arrange on warmed serving plates. Pour the sauce over the meat and garnish with the reserved cranberries and mint leaves. Serve with the Dauphinoise potatoes and purée of parsnips.

Demi Glace: Melt 25 g (1 oz) butter in a heavy-based pan. Add 1 chopped carrot and 1 chopped onion; fry gently until lightly browned. Stir in 25 g (1 oz) plain flour and cook, stirring, until browned. Gradually blend in 750 ml (1¼ pints) well-flavoured lamb stock. Add a bouquet garni and 10 ml (2 tsp) tomato purée. Cover and simmer for 1 hour, stirring frequently, until reduced and thickened. Strain through a fine sieve and check the seasoning. Use as required.

Pan-fried Lamb Cutlets with a Parmesan Crust, served with a Creamy Pesto Sauce

1 French-trimmed rack of lamb (with
    6 cutlets)
50 g (2 oz) Parmesan cheese, freshly grated
1 egg, lightly beaten
125 g (4 oz) fine, dry breadcrumbs
olive oil, for frying
salt and freshly ground black pepper

Pesto Sauce:
25 g (1 oz) basil leaves
1 clove garlic, crushed
25 g (1 oz) pine nuts, lightly toasted
5 ml (1 tsp) olive oil
25 g (1 oz) Parmesan cheese, freshly grated
125 ml (4 fl oz) whipping cream, or to taste
squeeze of lemon juice (optional)

To Serve:
Mustardy Baked Potatoes with Olives
    (see page 80)
shredded steamed green vegetables (baby
    asparagus, mangetout, courgettes,
    broccoli etc)

1   Cut the rack of lamb into cutlets. Turn the cutlets in the grated Parmesan to coat evenly on both sides, gently shaking off any excess cheese.

2   Immediately dip them in the beaten egg, then turn the cutlets in the breadcrumbs to coat all over.

3   To make the pesto sauce, put the basil leaves, garlic, pine nuts, olive oil and grated Parmesan in a blender or food processor and work to a rough paste; if difficult to blend, add a little water. Season with salt and pepper to taste. Blend in the cream, half at a time. Add a squeeze of lemon juice if wished, taking care to ensure the sauce does not curdle.

4   Approximately 10 minutes before serving, heat a 3 mm (⅛ inch) depth of olive oil in a heavy-based frying pan over a medium heat. Add the coated lamb cutlets and fry for 2-3 minutes until a golden brown crust has formed on the underside. Season with salt and pepper, turn the cutlets over and season again. Fry for a further 2-3 minutes to cook the other side.

5   Transfer the lamb cutlets to warmed plates and serve with the creamy pesto sauce and vegetable accompaniments.

Note: if required, the lamb cutlets can be prepared ahead to the end of stage 2, then refrigerated for 3-4 hours. However, they must be brought to room temperature before cooking.

Fillet of Lamb with a Port and Rosemary Sauce

2 lamb loin fillets, each about 200 g (7 oz)
a little oil, for cooking

Sauce:
1 shallot, chopped
150 ml (¼ pint) port
1 rosemary sprig
7.5 ml (1½ tsp) redcurrant jelly
squeeze of lemon juice
salt and freshly ground black pepper
175 ml (6 fl oz) light stock

To Serve:
Mushroom Medley (see page 64)
new potatoes
steamed patty pan squash

1 First make the sauce. Put the shallot, port, rosemary, redcurrant jelly, lemon juice and a little salt and pepper in a saucepan. Bring to the boil and reduce until syrupy. Pass through a fine sieve into another saucepan and add the stock. Boil again to reduce the sauce to a good consistency; set aside.

2 Lightly oil a heavy-based frying pan and preheat until very hot. Add the lamb and seal over a high heat on all sides.

3 Transfer the lamb to a baking dish and cook in a preheated oven at 200°C (400°F) mark 6 for 9 minutes.

4 Cover the lamb and leave to rest in a warm place for 6 minutes. In the meantime, reheat the sauce gently. Carve the meat into slices and arrange on warmed serving plates. Serve with the sauce and vegetable accompaniments.

Lamb Brochette with Spiced Chutney

The spiced chutney can be made up to 3 weeks in advance, cooled and stored in sterilized jars.

Lamb Brochettes:
250 g (9 oz) eye loin of lamb (Welsh lamb)
120 ml (8 tbsp) olive oil
30 ml (2 tbsp) chopped fresh rosemary
juice of 1 lemon
finely pared zest of 1 orange, cut into diamonds
salt and freshly ground black pepper
8 pitted prunes
4 shallots, halved
8 cherry tomatoes
4 bay leaves

Spiced Chutney:
60 g (2 oz) pitted prunes, chopped
150 ml (¼ pint) cider vinegar
230 g (8 oz) soft brown sugar
2.5 ml (½ tsp) mustard powder
pinch of ground cinnamon
pinch of cayenne pepper
230 g (8 oz) apples, peeled, cored and chopped
60 g (2 oz) seedless raisins
1 onion, chopped
145 g (5 oz) tomatoes, skinned and chopped

To Serve:
mashed potato flavoured with olive oil and chopped basil

1 To make the chutney, put all of the ingredients in a saucepan, bring to the boil, lower the heat and simmer, uncovered, for 30 minutes or until thick and syrupy. If you prefer a really thick chutney, cook for a further 5-10 minutes. Remove from the heat and set aside.

2 Cut the lamb into bite-size cubes. Place in a non-metallic bowl with the olive oil, rosemary, lemon juice and orange zest diamonds. Season generously with salt and pepper. Cover and leave to marinate in a cool place overnight, if possible.

3 Pre-soak 4 wooden skewers in hot water for 30 minutes.

4 To assemble the brochettes, remove the lamb and orange zest from the marinade, reserving the liquor. Thread the meat, orange zest, prunes, shallots and tomatoes alternately onto the wooden skewers, placing a bay leaf in the middle of each skewer.

5 Lay the brochettes on the grill rack, brush with the reserved marinade and cook under a preheated high grill for about 8 minutes, turning every 2 minutes. Serve at once, with the spiced chutney and flavoured mashed potato.

Braised Loin of Lamb on Root Vegetable Mash with Cranberry Chutney and Crispy Onion Rings

1 boned loin of lamb, about 250 g (9 oz)
7.5 ml (½ tbsp) olive oil
1 carrot, chopped
1 onion, chopped
300 ml (½ pint) homemade lamb stock
300 ml (½ pint) cranberry juice
15 ml (1 tbsp) cornflour, blended with
  30 ml (2 tbsp) water
1 bouquet garni
salt and freshly ground black pepper

Cranberry Chutney:
5 ml (1 tsp) oil
½ red onion, chopped
75 g (3 oz) cranberries
25 g (1 oz) brown sugar
2 cloves
10 ml (2 tsp) raspberry vinegar

Crispy Onion Rings:
1 red onion
150 ml (¼ pint) milk
plain flour, for coating
oil, for deep-frying

To Garnish:
few cranberries
rosemary sprigs

To Serve:
Root Vegetable Mash (see page 65)
Curly Kale with Sesame Seeds (see page 64)

1 Cut the lamb into 6 even-sized round pieces. Heat the olive oil in a heavy-based frying pan, add the lamb and fry briefly, turning to brown on all sides. Transfer to a casserole dish, using a slotted spoon.

2 Add the carrot and onion to the oil remaining in the pan and fry, stirring, until softened and lightly browned. Transfer to the casserole dish.

3 Add the lamb stock and cranberry juice to the frying pan, stirring to scrape up any sediment. Stir in the cornflour paste and cook, stirring, until is slightly thickened. Pour over the meat and vegetables, then add the bouquet garni and seasoning.

4 Cover and cook in a preheated oven at 200°C (400°F) mark 6 for 30 minutes. Lower the oven setting to 150°C (300°F) mark 2 and cook for a further 30 minutes.

5 In the meantime, make the chutney. Heat the oil in a small saucepan, add the onion and sweat gently until softened. Stir in the rest of the ingredients, bring to the boil and simmer, uncovered, for about 15 minutes until reduced and thickened.

6 Meanwhile make the onion rings. Slice the onion into rings, place in a bowl, pour on the milk and leave to stand for 5 minutes. Heat the oil in a deep-fat fryer. Drain the onion slices and toss in the flour to coat all over. Deep-fry in the hot oil for about 3 minutes until crisp and golden. Drain on kitchen paper.

7 To serve, spoon a portion of root vegetable mash onto each warmed serving plate. Arrange the lamb on the vegetable mash and top with the crispy onion rings. Pour some of the sauce around the plate, add a spoonful of cranberry chutney and garnish with a few cranberries and rosemary sprigs. Serve with the curly kale.

Spicy Lamb Kebab

30 ml (2 tbsp) milk
30 ml (2 tbsp) couscous
250 g (9 oz) lean minced lamb
½ onion, finely chopped
1 clove garlic, finely chopped
2.5 ml (½ tsp) ground allspice
2.5 ml (½ tsp) ground cumin
90-120 ml (6-8 tbsp/½ cup) finely chopped
    mixed fresh herbs (ie oregano, mint,
    parsley)
1 egg, beaten
salt and freshly ground black pepper
10 ml (2 tsp) olive oil

To Serve:
Courgette and Feta Pittas (see right)
Tabouleh (see page 84)
Greek-style yogurt
cayenne pepper, for sprinkling
Minted Potato and Peas (see page 70)

1 To make the kebabs, heat the milk in a microwave or saucepan, then pour over the couscous; leave to cool. As it cools, the couscous will absorb the liquid and fluff up.

2 In a mixing bowl, combine the minced lamb, onion, garlic, spices and chopped herbs. Mix well, then add the beaten egg, cooled couscous and seasoning to taste. Mix until thoroughly combined; the mixture should be quite sticky. Rinse your hands under cold water, then shape the mixture into 6 sausage shapes. Chill in the refrigerator until firm.

3 To cook the lamb kebabs, heat the olive oil in a large frying pan. Add the 'sausages' and fry, turning for about 15-20 minutes until brown and crispy. Drain on kitchen paper.

4 To serve, place a courgette and feta pitta in the middle of each warmed serving plate. Spoon on the tabouleh, then pile 3 kebabs on each portion. Top with a spoonful of yogurt and a sprinkling of cayenne. Place spoonfuls of the minted potato and peas around each pitta.

Courgette and Feta Pitta

These stuffed pittas are served with the Spicy Lamb Kebabs (see left).

Pitta Dough:

300 g (10 oz) plain flour
100 g (3½ oz) cornflour
2.5 ml (½ tsp) salt
250 ml (8 fl oz) cold water
cornflour, for dusting
melted butter, for brushing

Filling:

100 g (3½ oz) feta cheese
60 g (2¼ oz) spinach leaves
1 medium courgette
1 egg, lightly beaten
1.25 ml (¼ tsp) freshly grated nutmeg
salt and freshly ground black pepper

1 To make the pitta dough, sift the flour, cornflour and salt together into the food processor bowl. With the motor running, add half of the water in a steady stream through the feeder tube. Gradually add the rest of the water until the dough binds together and forms a ball.

2 Turn out onto a surface sprinkled liberally with cornflour and knead the dough for at least 10 minutes. Cover with a cloth and leave to stand for at least 1 hour.

3 To make the filling for the pittas, chop the feta cheese in the food processor; transfer to a mixing bowl. Repeat with the spinach leaves; add to the feta. Fit the grating disc and grate the courgette; leave in the food processor for 10 minutes, then remove, squeezing out excess moisture; add to the bowl of feta and spinach. Add the beaten egg, nutmeg and pepper to taste. Season lightly with salt if required, as feta cheese is quite salty. Mix well and set aside.

4 Pinch off a palm-sized piece of pastry dough and roll out as thinly as possible on a surface dusted with cornflour. Using a small bowl or plate as a guide, cut out a circle. Repeat to make 6 rounds of pastry in total.

5 Place two pastry rounds side by side on a lined and greased baking tray. Brush around the edges with melted butter, then spread a thin layer of filling on each round. Top each with another pastry circle, brush edges with butter, then add another layer of filling. Top with the final pastry rounds and brush all over with butter. Bake in a preheated oven at 190°C (375°F) mark 5 for 15-20 minutes until golden brown.

Medallions of Lamb and Pigeon Timbales on Potato Rösti with Wild Mushrooms and Lamb Jus

1 large best end of lamb fillet, or boned loin,
*   about 250 g (9 oz)*
salt and freshly ground black pepper
25 ml (1 fl oz) oil

Pigeon Timbales:
4 pigeon breasts
1 egg white
25 ml (1 fl oz) double cream
1 carrot, peeled
1 courgette

Rösti:
2 large potatoes

Jus:
300 ml (½ pint) well-flavoured lamb stock
50 g (2 oz) small wild mushrooms
25 g (1 oz) salted butter, diced
2 tomatoes, skinned, seeded and diced

To Garnish:
parsley sprigs
rosemary sprigs

1 Trim the lamb as necessary, cover and set aside.

2 Trim the pigeon breasts and place in a blender or food processor. Process until smooth, then blend in the egg white and cream. Season with salt and pepper. Spoon into a piping bag and chill in the refrigerator for about 20 minutes.

3 For the rösti, peel and grate the potatoes, then immerse in a bowl of cold water to remove excess starch. Drain thoroughly, squeeze dry and season with salt and pepper.

4 For the timbales, pare the carrot and courgette into long thin ribbons with a mandolin or swivel vegetable peeler. Line 2 buttered timbale moulds with the carrot and courgette ribbons, then pipe in the chilled pigeon mousseline. Cover the moulds with foil.

5 To cook the lamb, heat the oil in a heavy-based frying pan. Add the lamb and quickly sear over a high heat, turning to seal the meat on all sides. Transfer the lamb to a roasting tin and cook in a preheated oven at 200°C (400°F) mark 6 for 8 minutes.

6 At the same time, place the pigeon timbales in a steamer and steam for about 10 minutes.

7 Meanwhile, cook the rösti. Heat the oil remaining in the frying pan (the lamb was sealed in). Pack the grated potato into two 9 cm (3½ inch) metal rings, placed on a board. Carefully lift the rings into the hot frying pan, using a fish slice. Fry for 3-4 minutes, then turn the rösti and fry for a further 3-4 minutes until crisp and golden brown on both sides.

8 In the meantime, make the jus. Put the stock and wild mushrooms in a pan and bring to the boil. Let bubble to reduce and thicken. Whisk in the butter, then add the tomatoes.

9 Once the lamb is cooked, cover and leave to rest in a warm place for about 5 minutes.

10 To serve, place a rösti on each warmed serving plate. Carefully unmould the pigeon timbales and position on top of the rösti. Carve the lamb into medallions and arrange on the plates. Pour the lamb jus around the meat and garnish with herbs.

Lamb's Liver with Melted Onions and Marsala

30 ml (2 tbsp) olive oil
3 onions, halved and thinly sliced
1 large clove garlic, crushed
300 ml (½ pint) Marsala
30 ml (2 tbsp) balsamic vinegar
salt and freshly ground black pepper
225 g (8 oz) lamb's liver
15 g (½ oz) butter

To Serve:
Sliced Potatoes baked with Tomatoes and Basil (see page 78)

1 Heat 15 ml (1 tbsp) olive oil in a heavy-based frying pan, add the onions and fry, stirring, until evenly browned.

2 Add the garlic and sauté briefly, then pour in the Marsala and balsamic vinegar. Bring to a simmer, then lower the heat and let barely bubble for 45 minutes. Season with salt and pepper to taste.

3 Slice the liver into very thin strips. Heat the remaining 15 ml (1 tbsp) olive oil with the butter in another heavy-based frying pan. When the butter is foaming, add the liver slices and sear briefly for 1-2 minutes; do not overcook.

4 Transfer the liver to warmed serving plates. Pour on the hot Marsala sauce and onions and serve at once, with the potato accompaniment.

Garlic and Honey Pork

1 pork tenderloin, about 300 g (10 oz)
2.5 cm (1 inch) piece fresh root ginger,
* peeled and grated*
2 cloves garlic, crushed
30 ml (2 tbsp) thin honey
45 ml (3 tbsp) soy sauce
45 ml (3 tbsp) dry sherry
15 ml (1 tbsp) vegetable oil
30 ml (2 tbsp) sesame seeds

To Serve:
Vegetable Noodles (see page 60)

1 Trim the pork of any fat and membrane, then prick all over with a fork. Place in a small roasting dish.

2 Mix the ginger, garlic, honey, soy sauce, sherry and oil together in a bowl. Pour the mixture over the pork, to coat all over.

3 Roast in a preheated oven at 220°C (425°F) mark 7 for 15 minutes. Turn the pork over, baste with the cooking juices and sprinkle with the sesame seeds. Roast for a further 10 minutes, or until the pork is cooked through.

4 Cover the meat and leave to rest in a warm place for 10-15 minutes.

5 Carve the pork into thick slices. Arrange on warmed serving plates and spoon the cooking juices over the meat. Serve at once, with the vegetable noodles.

Steamed Pork Roll with Tomato and Pepper Stuffing

2 small, thin pork fillets, each about 150 g
  (5 oz)
4 tomatoes
10 ml (2 tsp) olive oil
½ onion, chopped
½ red pepper, seeded and chopped
1 clove garlic, finely chopped
5 basil leaves, chopped
salt and freshly ground black pepper

To Serve:
Potato Rösti (see page 69)
Ratatouille (see page 58)

1 If necessary, place each pork fillet between two sheets of greaseproof paper and beat with a rolling pin to flatten until the fillets are very thin.

2 Pierce the skin of each tomato in two or three places and immerse in a saucepan of boiling water for a few minutes, then remove from the water. Peel away the skins and finely chop the tomato flesh.

3 Heat the olive oil in a saucepan, add the onion and cook gently until softened, then add the red pepper, chopped tomato, garlic, basil and seasoning to taste. Simmer for 10-15 minutes until slightly reduced.

4 Transfer the mixture to a food processor and process briefly until finely chopped.

5 Lay the pork fillets flat on a clean surface and spoon about 45 ml (3 tbsp) of the tomato and pepper mixture on top of each one. Roll up to enclose the filling and tie at intervals with cotton string. Reserve the rest of the tomato mixture.

6 Place the pork rolls in a bamboo steamer over a pan of boiling water and season generously with salt and pepper. Cover and steam for about 15-20 minutes until cooked through.

7 Just before serving, reheat the rest of the tomato mixture. Remove the string from the pork rolls. Place a potato rösti on each serving plate and position a pork roll on top. Spoon on the reserved tomato mixture and serve with the ratatouille.

Cidered Fillet of Pork with Garlic and Sage

This meat should be marinated overnight.

1 pork tenderloin, about 300 g (10 oz)

Marinade:
15 ml (1 tbsp) dry cider
15 ml (1 tbsp) lemon juice
30 ml (2 tbsp) olive oil
5 ml (1 tsp) chopped sage
½ onion, chopped

Stuffing:
2 cloves garlic, crushed
4 mushrooms
6 dried apricots
15 ml (1 tbsp) chopped onion
grated zest and juice of 1 lemon
5 ml (½ tsp) chopped sage
salt and freshly ground black pepper
15 ml (1 tbsp) olive oil
15 ml (1 tbsp) fresh brown breadcrumbs

To Assemble:
6 rashers streaky bacon, derinded
15 ml (1 tbsp) olive oil
25 g (1 oz) butter
3 sheets filo pastry
beaten egg, for brushing
5 ml (1 tsp) vegetable gravy granules
60 ml (4 tbsp) dry cider
15 ml (1 tbsp) sherry or Calvados
10 ml (2 tsp) crème fraîche (optional)

To Serve:
Dressed Baby Carrots, Leeks and Mangetout
  (see page 56)
Potato Nests (see page 74)

1 Mix together the ingredients for the marinade in a shallow dish. Add the pork, spoon over the marinade and leave in a cool place overnight.

2 To make the stuffing, put the garlic, mushrooms, apricots, onion, lemon zest and juice, sage and seasoning in a blender or food processor and work briefly until evenly mixed. Heat the olive oil in a pan, add the mushroom mixture and cook over a low heat for about 10 minutes. Remove from the heat and mix in the breadcrumbs.

3 Remove pork from marinade and split horizontally without cutting all the way through, then open out like a book. Place the pork between two sheets of greaseproof paper and lightly flatten with a rolling pin; take care to avoid splitting the meat.

4 Spread the stuffing mixture along the middle of the pork, then bring the sides of the meat over the filling. Wrap the meat in the bacon rashers.

5 Heat the oil and butter in a heavy-based frying pan, add the pork and cook over a moderate heat for about 20 minutes, turning from time to time, until evenly browned on all sides. Remove from pan and let cool slightly; reserve the pan juices.

6 Lay the sheets of filo pastry one on top of another on a clean surface. Place the pork along one edge and roll up to wrap the pork in the filo pastry. Brush with beaten egg. Place on a baking tray and cook in a preheated oven at 220°C (400°F) mark 6 for 20 minutes until the pastry is crisp and golden brown.

7 About 5 minutes before the pork will be ready, reheat the reserved pan juices. Sprinkle in the gravy granules, then gradually mix in the cider and sherry or Calvados. Simmer gently and stir in the crème fraîche if using.

8 Carve the pork into thick slices. Arrange on warmed serving plates, pour over the sauce and serve with the vegetables.

Bacon-wrapped Pork Tenderloin filled with Pine Nuts, Sun-dried Tomatoes and Mushrooms

1 pork tenderloin, about 225 g (8 oz)
25 g (1 oz) butter
50 g (2 oz) mushrooms, wiped and finely
    chopped
2 sun-dried tomatoes, finely chopped, or
    5 ml (1 tsp) sun-dried tomato paste
15 ml (1 tbsp) pine nuts
25 g (1 oz) fresh white breadcrumbs
salt and freshly ground black pepper
4 bacon rashers, derinded
30 ml (2 tbsp) olive oil
5 ml (1 tsp) plain flour
60 ml (4 tbsp) port
15 ml (1 tbsp) tomato paste
150 ml (¼ pint) beef stock

To Garnish:
sage leaves

To Serve:
stir-fried winter vegetables (see note)
Creamed Potato Swirls with Herbs and
    Parmesan (see page 81)

1 Make a horizontal slit along the length of the pork, cutting only two-thirds of the way through.

2 Melt the butter in a small pan and fry the mushrooms, tomatoes and pine nuts for 2-3 minutes until softened. Remove from the heat and stir in the breadcrumbs and seasoning. Press the mixture into the slit in the pork.

3 Stretch each rasher of bacon with the back of a knife and wrap around the pork tightly to enclose the filling. Secure with a cocktail stick at each end.

4 Lay the pork in a small roasting tin, brush with the olive oil and roast in a preheated oven at 190°C (375°F) mark 5 for 30 minutes. Lift the pork out of the tin and leave to rest on a warmed plate while preparing the gravy.

5 Pour the pan juices into a small saucepan and sprinkle the flour over. Cook gently for a few seconds, then gradually add the port, tomato paste and stock. Cook, stirring, until you have a smooth gravy; check the seasoning.

6 To serve, carve the pork into slices and arrange on warmed serving plates. Drizzle with a little of the gravy. Garnish with sage leaves and serve with the vegetables. Hand the remaining gravy separately.

Note: Use a mixture of vegetables, such as carrots, white cabbage and parsnips. For optimum effect, serve them in puff pastry cornets.

Wiltshire Ham, served with a Mushroom and Madeira Sauce

The weight of ham in this recipe is more than required to serve 2 but it isn't practical to cook less. Any leftover meat will be delicious served cold.

1 small piece of slipper of Wiltshire ham,
  about 450 g (1 lb)
20 g (¾ oz) butter
4 spring onions (white part only), trimmed
  and chopped
20 g (¾ oz) plain flour
100 ml (3½ fl oz) light stock (see below)
100 ml (3½ fl oz) Madeira
80 g (3 oz) closed cup mushrooms, chopped
100 ml (3½ fl oz) single cream

To Serve:
Creamed Spinach with Nutmeg
  (see page 63)
Isosceles Roast Potatoes (see page 71)

1 Place the ham in a saucepan in which it fits quite snugly. Add sufficient water to cover and bring to the boil. Lower the heat, cover and simmer for about 25 minutes until tender.

2 Meanwhile heat the butter in a saucepan, add the spring onions and cook gently until softened but not browned. Stir in the flour and cook gently for 1 minute.

3 Bring the stock and Madeira to a simmer in a separate pan. Gradually add to the flour and onion mixture, stirring thoroughly after each addition to ensure no lumps form.

4 Bring the sauce to simmering point, stirring constantly, then add the mushrooms and cook for 5 minutes until tender. Reduce the heat and stir in the cream; do not allow to boil or the mixture will curdle.

5 Drain the ham and slice very thinly; arrange in the centre of warmed serving plates. Using a slotted spoon, spoon some of the sauce over the ham. Serve at once, with the spinach and roast potatoes. Serve the remainder of the sauce separately, in a sauceboat.

Note: For the stock, use 1 carrot, 1 small onion, 1 stick celery, 1 leek, 1 parsnip and 1 bouquet garni. Cut the vegetables into large chunks, place in a saucepan with the bouquet garni and add cold water to cover. Bring to the boil and simmer for about 40 minutes. Season with salt and pepper to taste. Strain through a fine sieve, then use as required.

Vegetarian Dishes

Spiced Carrot Tart with Sweet Potato Pastry

Pastry:
75 g (3 oz) sweet potato, peeled and cut into chunks
75 g (3 oz) plain flour
2.5 ml (½ tsp) baking powder
salt and freshly ground black pepper
40 g (1½ oz) unsalted butter, in pieces
a little beaten egg, for brushing

Filling:
1 large carrot, peeled and halved
25 g (1 oz) white bread, crusts removed
1 egg, beaten
100 g (3½ oz) creamed coconut (½ packet)
75 ml (2½ fl oz) boiling water
1 cm (½ inch) piece fresh root ginger, peeled and grated
large pinch of ground cumin
15 ml (1 tbsp) ground coriander
30 ml (2 tbsp) chopped fresh coriander
10 ml (2 tsp) lemon juice

To Serve:
coriander sprigs, to garnish
Stir-fried Vegetables (see page 55)

1 Place the sweet potato (for the pastry) and the carrot (for the filling) in a saucepan. Add cold water to cover and bring to the boil. Lower the heat and simmer for 5 minutes. Remove the carrot and cook the sweet potato for a further 10 minutes or until soft. Drain and mash the sweet potato.

2 To make the pastry, sift the flour, baking powder and seasoning together and place in the food processor bowl. Add the butter and process briefly until well rubbed in. Transfer to a bowl and cut in the mashed sweet potato, using a round-bladed knife. Work the dough together, using your fingers.

3 Grease and flour two 10 cm (4 inch) individual fluted flan tins. Divide the pastry in half. Roll out each piece to a thin round and use to line each tin. Prick the base well and brush with a little beaten egg. Transfer to a preheated baking sheet and bake in the preheated oven at 200°C (400°F) mark 6 for 15 minutes or until crisp. Remove from the oven and lower the oven temperature to 180°C (350°F) mark 4.

4 To make the filling, grate the parboiled carrot into a bowl. Break the bread into pieces and process to breadcrumbs in the food processor. Add to the carrot. Stir in the beaten egg.

5 Put the creamed coconut in a jug, add the boiling water and stir to dissolve. Add the coconut to the carrot mixture with the ginger, spices, chopped coriander, lemon juice and plenty of seasoning.

6 Pour the filling into the pre-baked pastry cases and arrange a decorative sprig of coriander on top. Bake in the oven for 15-20 minutes or until the filling is set and firm. Serve at once, accompanied by the stir-fried vegetables.

Accompaniments

Lamb's Leaf Salad with a Raspberry Vinaigrette

75 g (3 oz) lamb's lettuce

Dressing:
10 ml (2 tsp) raspberry wine vinegar
30 ml (2 tbsp) olive oil
5 ml (1 tsp) Dijon mustard
salt and freshly ground black pepper
pinch of sugar, to taste

1 Whisk the ingredients for the dressing together in a bowl, or shake in a screw-topped jar, until evenly combined.

2 Trim the salad leaves; rinse and dry if necessary. Arrange on individual serving plates and drizzle over the dressing to serve.

Stir-fried Sugar Snap Peas and Cucumber

½ cucumber
125 g (4 oz) sugar snap peas
15 ml (1 tbsp) olive oil
sea salt

1 Peel the cucumber, then quarter lengthwise. Remove the seeds, then cut the cucumber flesh into 5 cm (2 inch) batons. Set aside.

2 Cut the sugar snap peas in half diagonally.

3 Heat the olive oil in a frying pan until very hot. Add the sugar snap peas and cucumber and stir-fry for 30 seconds only.

4 Take off the heat and sprinkle with a little freshly milled sea salt. Serve at once.

Stir-fried Vegetables

125 g (4 oz) sugar snap peas
½ red pepper, seeded
½ yellow pepper, seeded
1 large courgette, halved
3 spring onions, trimmed
¼ head Chinese leaves
5 ml (1 tsp) soy sauce
5 ml (1 tsp) lemon juice
5 ml (1 tsp) sunflower oil
salt and freshly ground black pepper

1 Trim the sugar snap peas, if necessary. Cut the peppers into thin strips. Using a swivel vegetable peeler, pare the courgette into ribbons along its length. Chop the spring onions, using as much of the green part as possible. Finely shred the Chinese leaves. Mix the soy sauce and lemon juice together in a small bowl.

2 Heat the oil in a wok until it is very hot. Add the pepper strips and stir-fry for 1 minute. Add the sugar snap peas and continue to stir-fry until they are beginning to soften.

3 Toss in the courgette ribbons and spring onions. Cook, stirring, for a few seconds, keeping the heat high.

4 Quickly pour in the soy and lemon juice mixture, then immediately add the Chinese leaves, to cook in the steam. Put the lid on the wok for a few seconds until the Chinese leaves are just wilting and warmed through. Season generously with salt and pepper. Serve at once

Dressed Baby Carrots, Leeks and Mangetout

10 baby carrots
finely grated zest and juice of ½ lemon
15 g (½ oz) butter
5 ml (1 tsp) sugar
salt and freshly ground black pepper
4 small leeks, trimmed
50-75 g (2-3 oz) mangetout

1 Place the carrots in a saucepan, pour on enough cold water to just cover, then add the lemon zest and juice, butter, sugar, salt and pepper.

2 Bring to the boil, lower the heat and simmer for 2-3 minutes. Add the leeks and mangetout. Continue cooking until the vegetables are al dente, tender but firm to the bite.

3 Drain thoroughly and serve.

Stir-fried Vegetable Bundles

1 carrot, peeled
10 baby corn cobs
10 mangetout
1 courgette
15 ml (1 tbsp) sesame oil
1 clove garlic, crushed
2.5 ml (½ tsp) crushed fresh root ginger
dash of balsamic vinegar

To Serve:
strips of leek, blanched

1 Cut the carrot, baby corn, mangetout and courgette into julienne 'matchstick strips'.

2 Heat the sesame oil in a wok or heavy-based frying pan. Add the garlic and ginger and stir-fry briefly until golden.

3 Toss in the vegetable julienne and stir-fry until lightly browned and just tender. Add a dash of balsamic vinegar.

4 Tie in bundles using strips of blanched leek. Serve at once.

Ratatouille

2 courgettes, chopped
½ aubergine, chopped
salt and freshly ground black pepper
10 ml (2 tsp) olive oil
½ onion, chopped
3 tomatoes, skinned and chopped
½ red pepper, seeded and chopped
10 ml (2 tsp) tomato paste

1 Sprinkle the chopped courgettes and aubergine liberally with salt and leave to degorge for 20 minutes. Rinse thoroughly to remove the salt and pat dry with kitchen paper.

2 Heat the oil in a large saucepan, add the onion and cook gently until softened. Add the chopped tomatoes and allow to gently simmer for 10 minutes.

3 Add the red pepper and courgette and cook for 10 minutes, then add the aubergine, tomato paste and seasoning to taste. Simmer for 15 minutes until all the vegetables are tender. Serve hot.

Layered Vegetables

200-225 g (7-8 oz) carrots, peeled
200-225 g (7-8 oz) courgettes, trimmed
175-225 g (6-8 oz) leek, trimmed
½ onion, finely chopped
salt and freshly ground black pepper

1 Thinly slice the carrots, courgettes and leek into rounds.

2 Layer the vegetables in two buttered dariole moulds, starting with a layer of carrot, then a little chopped onion, then a layer of leek slices, a little more onion and finally a layer of courgette; season each layer with salt and pepper. Repeat the layers to fill the dariole moulds. Cover each one with a piece of buttered foil.

3 Stand the dariole moulds in a roasting tin half-filled with boiling water. Cook in a preheated oven at 180°C (350°F) mark 4 for 45-50 minutes until the vegetables are tender. Turn out the layered vegetables onto warmed plates to serve.

Vegetable Noodles

½ yellow or green pepper, seeded
2 spring onions, trimmed
1 lemon grass stalk
100 g (3½ oz) beansprouts
grated zest and juice of ½ lemon
15 ml (1 tbsp) sesame oil
50 g (2 oz) Chinese egg noodles
30 ml (2 tbsp) vegetable oil

To Garnish:
sesame seeds, for sprinkling
spring onion tassels (see note)

1 Finely slice the pepper. Slice the spring onions diagonally. Remove and discard the outer leaves from the lemon grass stalk, then shred finely. Rinse and drain the beansprouts in a large colander.

2 In a bowl, mix the lemon zest and juice with the sesame oil.

3 Add the noodles to a large pan of boiling water and boil for 4 minutes.

4 Meanwhile, heat the vegetable oil in a wok or sauté pan. Add the pepper, spring onions and lemon grass, and stir-fry for 1 minute.

5 Drain the noodles through the beansprouts in the colander, then add both to the stir-fry.

6 Add the lemon and sesame oil mixture and stir-fry briefly. Serve garnished with a sprinkling of sesame seeds and the spring onion tassels.

Note: To make spring onion tassels, trim off the base and dark green part. Using a sharp knife, shred the spring onion lengthwise, leaving about 2.5 cm (1 inch) of the bulb end intact. Immerse in a bowl of iced water for about 30 minutes until opened out. Drain well.

Citrus Leeks with Sugar Snap Peas

250 g (9 oz) trimmed leeks
10 ml (2 tsp) olive oil
150 g (5 oz) sugar snap peas, trimmed
salt and freshly ground black pepper

Dressing:
25 ml (5 tsp) olive oil
5 ml (1 tsp) balsamic vinegar
2.5 ml (½ tsp) light brown sugar
5 ml (1 tsp) lemon juice
2.5 ml (½ tsp) Dijon mustard
finely grated zest and juice of ½ orange

1 Cut the leeks into 1 cm (½ inch) chunks.

2 Heat the oil in a large sauté pan, add the leeks and sauté gently for 5-6 minutes or until just tender.

3 Meanwhile cook the sugar snap peas in boiling salted water for 3-5 minutes. Drain thoroughly, then toss with the leeks.

4 Whisk together all the ingredients for the dressing and season with salt and pepper to taste. Pour the dressing over the hot vegetables and toss to mix. Serve immediately.

Crunchy-topped Leeks

1 large leek, trimmed
salt
75 g (3 oz) brown breadcrumbs
25 g (1 oz) Cheddar cheese, grated

1 Thinly slice the leek and cook in boiling salted water for about 5 minutes until just tender. Drain well.

2 Transfer the leek to a gratin dish. Mix the breadcrumbs and grated cheese together and sprinkle evenly over the leek. Cook under a preheated high grill until the topping is crisp and golden brown. Serve immediately.

Mixed Pepper Stir-fry

½ red pepper, seeded
½ green pepper, seeded
½ yellow pepper, seeded
1 carrot, peeled
15 ml (1 tbsp) sesame oil
salt and freshly ground black pepper

1 Slice the peppers and carrot into julienne (matchstick strips).

2 Heat the sesame oil in a wok or frying pan. Add the vegetable julienne and cook over a high heat for a few minutes until *al dente*, tender but still firm to the bite. Season with salt and pepper to taste.

3 Transfer to warmed serving plates, arranging the vegetables in a lattice pattern. Serve at once.

Caramelised Roasted Garlic Spinach

40 ml (2½ tbsp) groundnut oil
2 plump garlic cloves, partially crushed
200 g (7 oz) packet ready-prepared young
* spinach leaves*
salt and freshly ground black pepper

1 Heat the groundnut oil in a large heavy-based saucepan until very hot. Add the garlic cloves and toss in the hot oil for 1-2 minutes until caramelised.

2 Add the spinach and cook for 1-1½ minutes until just starting to wilt. Drain thoroughly and discard the garlic cloves.

3 Season with salt and pepper to taste. Serve at once.

Creamed Spinach with Nutmeg

400 g (14 oz) spinach leaves, trimmed
50 ml (2 fl oz) single cream
freshly grated nutmeg, to taste
salt and freshly ground black pepper

1 Bring a little water to the boil in a saucepan, then add the spinach. Cover and cook for about 1 minute. Turn the spinach leaves and cook for a further 30 seconds.

2 Immediately drain in a colander, pressing with the back of a wooden spoon to remove as much liquid as possible.

3 Return the spinach to the pan, add the cream and season with nutmeg, salt and pepper to taste. Reheat gently and serve.

Curly Kale with Sesame Seeds

125 g (4 oz) curly kale
salt and freshly ground black pepper
25 g (1 oz) butter, melted
15 g (½ oz) sesame seeds

1 Cook the curly kale in boiling salted water for 3-5 minutes. Drain thoroughly and return to the pan.

2 Add the melted butter and sesame seeds and toss to mix. Serve at once.

Mushroom Medley

15 g (½ oz) butter
1 shallot, finely chopped
125 g (4 oz) chestnut mushrooms, sliced
salt and freshly ground black pepper
snipped chives, to garnish

1 Heat the butter in a frying pan. Add the chopped shallot and sweat gently until quite soft and transparent.

2 Add the mushrooms and fry quickly over a fairly high heat for 1-2 minutes. Drain on kitchen paper.

3 Season with salt and pepper and serve garnished with snipped chives.

Celeriac and Apple Purée

½ celeriac bulb, about 300 g (10 oz)
½ Bramley apple, about 100 g (3½ oz)
large knob of butter
salt and freshly ground black pepper

1 Peel the celeriac and cut into cubes. Steam for approximately 15 minutes or until almost tender.

2 Meanwhile, peel, core and roughly chop the apple. Add to the steamer with the par-cooked celeriac and cook for a further 5 minutes or until both are tender.

3 Transfer to a warmed bowl, add the butter and seasoning and mash until smooth. Serve piping hot.

Root Vegetable Mash

1 potato
1 turnip
1 carrot
1 parsnip
½ sweet potato
salt and freshly ground black pepper
large knob of butter
15 ml (1 tbsp) chopped parsley

1 Peel the vegetables and cut into even-sized pieces.

2 Add the potato to a pan of cold salted water, bring to the boil and cook for about 5 minutes.

3 Add the other root vegetables to the pan and cook until tender. Drain thoroughly.

4 Return the vegetables to the pan, add the butter, parsley and seasoning and mash until smooth. Serve piping hot.

Garlic Acorn Squash

1 acorn squash
50 g (2 oz) butter, softened
1 clove garlic, crushed
salt and freshly ground black pepper

1 Quarter and peel the squash. Make deep slashes in each quarter of squash at 2.5 cm (1 inch) intervals, without cutting right through.

2 Mix the butter and crushed garlic together in a bowl. Spread the garlic butter into the slits in the squash (as for garlic bread).

3 Put the squash quarters on a baking tray and bake in a preheated oven at 180°C (350°F) mark 4 for 30 minutes.

4 Transfer the squash to a bowl and mash until smooth. Season with salt and pepper to taste. Serve piping hot.

Purée of Parsnips

500 g (1 lb 2 oz) parsnips
salt and freshly ground black pepper
75 ml (5 tbsp) double cream
20 g (¾ oz) butter
10 ml (2 tsp) black poppy seeds

1 Peel and slice the parsnips, discarding the woody cores. Place in a suitable dish with a little salted water, cover and microwave on HIGH for 6 minutes.

2 Drain the parsnips and place in a food processor with the cream and butter. Process briefly until just smooth, then check the seasoning and gently stir in the poppy seeds. Serve piping hot.

Note: If preferred, the parsnips can be cooked in a saucepan with the minimum of water until softened, rather than in the microwave. They may also be mashed by hand, rather than processed, until smooth.

Colcannon

175 g (6 oz) King Edwards potatoes
salt and freshly ground black pepper
125 g (4 oz) Savoy cabbage
30 ml (2 tbsp) chopped chives
25 g (1 oz) butter
30 ml (2 tbsp) whipping cream

1 Peel and roughly chop the potatoes. Place in a pan of cold salted water, bring to the boil and cook until tender.

2 Meanwhile, core and shred the cabbage. Cook in boiling salted water until *al dente*, tender but still firm to the bite; drain thoroughly.

3 Drain the potatoes and return to the pan; mash smoothly. Add the cooked cabbage, chives, butter and cream. Toss to mix and season with salt and pepper to taste. Serve piping hot.

Potato and Apple Rösti

1 baking potato
1 Granny Smith apple
15 ml (1 tbsp) melted butter
salt and freshly ground black pepper
pinch of freshly grated nutmeg

1 Peel and grate the potato. Peel, core and grate the apple. Place the grated potato and apple on a clean tea-towel and squeeze gently to dry, then place in a bowl.

2 Mix in the melted butter and season with salt, pepper and the nutmeg. Divide the mixture into two portions.

3 Preheat a heavy-based frying pan. Add the rösti, shaping them into cakes and flatten slightly. Cook for about 5 minutes or until golden brown, then turn them over and cook until the other side is golden brown. Serve piping hot.

Potato and Parsnip Rösti

1 large potato
1 parsnip
25 g (1 oz) butter
½ onion, finely chopped
salt and freshly ground black pepper
15 ml (1 tbsp) chopped mixed herbs
  (eg parsley, oregano, basil)

1 Prick the skin of the potato and parsnip. Place on a baking sheet and roast in a preheated oven at 200°C (400°F) mark 6 for approximately 20 minutes, until half-cooked. Leave to cool.

2 Heat the butter in a small pan, add the onion and fry gently until softened but not browned.

3 Remove the skin from the potato and parsnip. Coarsely grate the potato and parsnip flesh and add to the onion. Season with salt and pepper and stir in the chopped herbs.

4 Spoon the mixture into two greased 7.5 cm (3 inch) metal ring moulds, pressing well down. Bake in the oven at 180°C (350°F) mark 4 for approximately 15 minutes. Serve piping hot.

Potato Rösti

2 potatoes
salt and freshly ground black pepper
freshly grated nutmeg, to taste
1-2 rosemary sprigs, leaves only
oil, for frying

1 Peel and grate the potatoes and season with salt, pepper and nutmeg. Add the chopped rosemary.

2 Heat a film of oil in a heavy-based frying pan until very hot. Divide the potato into two portions and squeeze out any excess liquid.

3 Carefully place both potato portions in the pan, spacing them well apart. Using the back of a spoon, spread out to form two pancakes, each 10-12 cm (4-5 inches) in diameter. Cook over a moderate heat for 4-5 minutes each side until golden brown and crisp.

4 Drain the rösti on kitchen paper and serve.

Minted Mustardy Potato and Peas

15 ml (1 tbsp) olive oil
2.5 ml (½ tsp) brown mustard seeds
½ onion, roughly chopped
1 large potato, peeled and cut into 1 cm
    (½ inch) cubes
2.5 ml (½ tsp) turmeric
2.5 ml (½ tsp) dried mint
75 g (3 oz) frozen peas
garam masala, to taste

1   Heat the olive oil in a small saucepan or sauté pan, add the mustard seeds and fry over a moderate heat until they start to pop.

2   Add the onion, potato, turmeric and mint and fry gently until lightly coloured. Add enough water to cover the potatoes and simmer over a low heat for 15 minutes or until the potatoes are cooked through, topping up the water if required.

3   Add the peas and cook for a further 5 minutes until they are tender, and most of the liquid is evaporated.

4   Just before serving, sprinkle with garam masala to taste.

Isosceles Roast Potatoes

2 large potatoes
50 g (2 oz) lard
salt and freshly ground black pepper

1 Peel the potatoes, halve lengthwise and slice very thinly. Trim each half slice into a triangular shape, with fairly even sides.

2 Place the potato triangles in a small saucepan, add cold water to cover and bring to the boil. Cover and simmer for about 2½ minutes; drain.

3 Meanwhile, put the lard in a baking tin and place in a preheated oven at 200°C (400°F) mark 6.

4 Add the potato triangles to the hot lard and bake in the oven for 10 minutes. Turn the slices over and return to the oven for a further 10 minutes, or until they are golden and crispy.

5 Immediately remove from the fat and drain on kitchen paper. Season with salt and pepper and serve piping hot.

Champ

350 g (12 oz) potatoes
salt and freshly ground black pepper
100 ml (3½ fl oz) full-cream milk
large knob of butter
2 large spring onions, trimmed and finely
  chopped

1 Peel and quarter the potatoes. Place in a large pan and add cold salted water to cover. Bring to the boil, lower the heat and simmer for 20 minutes, or until just cooked. Pour off the water and let stand for 3 minutes.

2 Combine the milk and butter in a pan and bring to the boil. Add the chopped spring onions to the boiling mixture, then remove from the heat.

3 Mash the potatoes and stir in the milk mixture, mashing until smooth. Check the seasoning. Serve piping hot.

Note: As you serve the champ, make a shallow hollow in the middle to hold a generous knob of butter.

Basil-fried Potato Balls

3 medium potatoes
salt
40 g (1½ oz) wholemeal breadcrumbs
7.5 ml (1½ tsp) chopped basil
1 egg, beaten
15 ml (1 tbsp) virgin olive oil

1 Add the potatoes to a pan of cold salted water, bring to the boil and par-boil for 10-12 minutes. Drain thoroughly. When cool enough to handle, use a melon baller to scoop the potato flesh into small balls.

2 Mix the breadcrumbs and chopped basil together and spread out on a plate.

3 Dip the potato balls into the beaten egg, then roll in the crumb mixture to coat all over.

4 Heat the oil in a frying pan. Add the potato balls and fry for 10 minutes, stirring occasionally, until evenly browned. Drain on kitchen paper and serve.

Potato Nests

200 g (7 oz) baby new potatoes
salt and freshly ground black pepper
10 ml (2 tsp) chopped parsley
30 ml (2 tbsp) crème fraîche
30 ml (2 tbsp) mayonnaise
2.5 ml (½ tsp) wholegrain mustard
2.5 ml (½ tsp) Dijon mustard

1 Put the potatoes in a saucepan, cover with cold water and bring to the boil. Lower the heat and simmer, covered, for approximately 8 minutes until cooked, but still firm. Drain thoroughly.

2 Return the potatoes to the pan, add all the other ingredients and toss well.

3 Spoon into warmed 7.5 cm (3 inch) metal ring moulds, then turn out onto warmed serving plates to form nests.

Scalloped Potatoes

4 small-medium potatoes, peeled
½ onion, sliced
20 g (¾ oz) plain flour
25 g (1 oz) butter
salt and freshly ground black pepper
150 ml (¼ pint) milk (approximately)

1 Grease a 15 cm (6 inch) square baking dish. Cut the potatoes into thin slices.

2 Arrange a third of the potato slices in the baking dish, then scatter over half of the onion slices and sprinkle with half of the flour. Dot with butter and season with plenty of salt and pepper. Repeat these layers once more, then cover with the remaining potato slices.

3 Pour in enough milk so that it is just visible through the top layer of potato slices. Cover with foil and cook in a preheated oven at 200°C (400°F) mark 6 for 45 minutes. Remove the foil and cook for a further 30 minutes or until the potatoes are tender and golden brown. Serve piping hot.

Almond Potatoes

225 g (8 oz) potatoes
large knob of butter
salt and freshly ground black pepper
1 small egg, beaten
seasoned flour, for coating
100 g (4 oz) nibbed almonds
oil, for deep-frying

1 Peel the potatoes and cook in boiling salted water for 15-20 minutes until soft; drain well.

2 Mash the potatoes with the butter and season with salt and pepper to taste. Add half of the beaten egg and beat well until evenly incorporated.

3 When cool enough to handle, divide the potato into small balls of equal size. Roll in seasoned flour to coat evenly, then dip into the rest of the beaten egg and finally into the nibbed almonds. Place on a plate and leave in the refrigerator until required.

4 When ready to serve, heat the oil for deep-frying in a suitable pan. When hot, deep-fry the potato balls until crisp and golden. Drain on kitchen paper and serve.

Potato Gratin

2 large potatoes (unpeeled)
7.5 ml (½ tbsp) olive oil
1 clove garlic, crushed
pinch of dried mixed herbs
salt and freshly ground black pepper
50 g (2 oz) gruyère cheese, grated

1 Mix the olive oil with the crushed garlic, herbs and seasoning.

2 Thinly slice the potatoes and layer in two lightly greased ramekin dishes, brushing each layer with the olive oil mixture.

3 Sprinkle the grated cheese over the top and par-cook in the microwave on HIGH for 3 minutes. Transfer to a preheated oven at 200°C (400°F) mark 6 and cook for approximately 30 minutes until tender.

4 Run a knife around the edge of each ramekin and underneath the potatoes. Carefully transfer to warmed serving plates, cheese-side up. Serve at once.

Sliced Potatoes baked with Tomatoes and Basil

450 g (1 lb) potatoes
salt and freshly ground black pepper
½ onion, finely chopped
225 g (8 oz) ripe tomatoes, skinned, seeded
  and chopped
1 plump clove garlic, crushed
20-25 ml (1½ tbsp) basil leaves
15 ml (1 tbsp) virgin olive oil

1 Parboil the potatoes in salted water for 10 minutes; drain and leave until cool enough to handle. Peel away the skins and cut into thin slices.

2 Arrange a third of the potato slices in a layer in the base of two 9 cm (3½ inch) metal rings.

3 Cover with half of the onion, tomatoes, garlic and basil. Season with salt and pepper.

4 Arrange another third of the potatoes on top, in an overlapping layer, then cover with the remaining onion, tomatoes, garlic and basil. Season and top with the rest of the potato slices.

5 Heat the olive oil in a frying pan until hot. Using a fish slice, slide the potato cakes into the pan in their rings and fry for approximately 2-3 minutes until golden brown underneath.

6 Invert into a shallow baking tin and bake in a preheated oven at 190°C (375°F) mark 5 for approximately 15 minutes until the potatoes are tender. Carefully press the potato cakes out of the tins to serve.

Dauphinoise Potatoes

500 g (1 lb 2 oz) potatoes
salt and freshly ground black pepper
freshly grated nutmeg
1 egg, beaten
375 ml (13 fl oz) double cream
65 g (2½ oz) Gruyère cheese, grated
1 clove garlic, halved
20 g (¾ oz) butter

1 Peel and thinly slice the potatoes. Place in a bowl and season with salt, pepper and grated nutmeg. Add the beaten egg, cream and half of the grated cheese; mix well.

2 Rub a shallow ovenproof dish with the cut garlic clove, then butter generously. Spoon the potato mixture into the prepared dish and sprinkle the surface liberally with the rest of the grated cheese and flaked butter.

3 Cook in a preheated oven at 180°C (350°F) mark 4 for 40 minutes, or until the potatoes are tender. Serve piping hot.

Individual Potatoes Dauphinoise

1 large potato, weighing 225-300 g
  (8-10 oz)
15 g (½ oz) unsalted butter
¼ clove garlic, crushed
salt and freshly ground black pepper
60 ml (4 tbsp) double cream

1 Butter two individual gratin dishes. Peel the potato and slice thinly.

2 Put the butter in a saucepan with the garlic and melt slowly.

3 Layer the potato slices neatly in each gratin dish, brushing each layer with the butter and garlic, and seasoning with salt and pepper.

4 Pour the cream over the top layer of potatoes.

5 Cover the dishes with buttered foil and bake in a preheated oven at 180°C (350°F) mark 4 for 45 minutes to 1 hour, until soft in the centre and golden on top.

Mustardy Baked Potatoes with Olives

2 large potatoes
30 ml (2 tbsp) olive oil
½ onion, finely chopped
1 clove garlic, finely chopped
5 ml (1 tsp) black mustard seeds
7.5 ml (1½ tsp) Dijon mustard
7.5 ml (1½ tsp) dried Italian herbs
30 ml (2 tbsp) chopped pitted black olives

1 Peel the potatoes and cut into 2 cm (¾ inch) cubes.

2 Heat the olive oil in a heavy-based saucepan. Add the potatoes, onion, garlic, mustard seeds, Dijon mustard and herbs. Stir over the heat until combined.

3 Transfer the mixture to an ovenproof dish. Bake, uncovered, in a preheated oven at 200°C (400°F) mark 6 for 30 minutes, stirring occasionally.

4 Stir in the olives and bake, uncovered, for a further 30 minutes or until the potatoes are crisp. Serve piping hot.

Creamed Potato Swirls with Herbs and Parmesan

350 g (12 oz) peeled potatoes
45 ml (3 tbsp) crème fraîche
1 egg yolk
30 ml (2 tbsp) ground almonds
15 ml (1 tbsp) chopped parsley
25 g (1 oz) Parmesan cheese, freshly grated
salt and freshly ground black pepper

1 Add the potatoes to a pan of lightly salted water. Bring to the boil, lower the heat and cook until tender. Drain the potatoes and let cool for 5 minutes.

2 Add the crème fraîche, egg yolk, ground almonds, parsley and Parmesan to the potatoes and mash smoothly. Season with salt and pepper to taste.

3 Spoon into a piping bag and pipe rosettes or swirls of potato on to a lightly oiled baking sheet. Bake in a preheated oven at 190°C (375°F) mark 5 for about 20 minutes until golden brown.

Rice Noodles with Shiitake Mushrooms and Oyster Sauce

75 g (3 oz) rice stick noodles
15 ml (1 tbsp) oil
25 g (1 oz) shiitake mushrooms, sliced
10 ml (2 tsp) oyster sauce
salt and freshly ground black pepper

1 Place the rice noodles in a pan of boiling water and cook for 6 minutes, or according to packet instructions. Drain, refresh in cold water and drain thoroughly.

2 Heat the oil in a wok or frying pan, add the mushrooms and stir-fry briefly. Add the noodles and oyster sauce and stir-fry for about 1 minute until heated through.

3 Check the seasoning and serve at once.

Japanese Rice

200 g (7 oz) Japanese glutinous rice
22 ml (1½ tbsp) rice wine vinegar
7.5 ml (1½ tsp) caster sugar
2.5 ml (½ tsp) salt

To Garnish:
toasted sesame seeds
nori (optional), finely shredded

1 Cook the rice according to the packet instructions. Drain thoroughly. Mix the vinegar, sugar and salt together in a small bowl to make a dressing.

2 Form the rice into mounds on the warmed serving plates and drizzle over the dressing.

3 Sprinkle with toasted sesame seeds and garnish with the shredded seaweed if using. Serve at once.

Note: Nori is a type of Japanese seaweed obtainable from oriental food stores.

Timbale of Mixed Rice

50 g (2 oz) long-grain brown rice
10 g (⅓ oz) wild rice
salt and freshly ground black pepper
15 ml (1 tbsp) olive oil
10 g (⅓ oz) pine nuts
30-45 ml (2-3 tbsp) chopped parsley, to taste

1 Cook the brown and wild rice in boiling salted water until tender (see note).

2 Drain the rice in a sieve and rinse with boiling water. Drain thoroughly and transfer to a heated dish.

3 Stir in the oil and season with salt and pepper to taste. Stir in the toasted pine nuts and plenty of chopped parsley.

4 Pack the rice into warmed dariole moulds, then turn out onto warmed plates to serve.

Note: The brown and wild rice can be cooked together but refer to the recommended cooking time on the packet directions. You may need to start cooking the wild rice first.

Tabouleh

65 g (2½ oz) bulghar wheat
125 ml (4 fl oz) boiling water
2 spring onions, chopped
2 tomatoes, seeded and chopped
¼ cucumber, seeded and chopped
handful of parsley, finely chopped
juice of ½ lemon
salt and freshly ground black pepper

1 Put the bulghar wheat in a bowl, pour on the boiling water and set aside to cool. As it cools the bulghar wheat will absorb the water and fluff up.

2 Once cooled, drain off any excess water, then add the spring onions, tomatoes, cucumber and parsley. Add the lemon juice, season with salt and pepper to taste and toss thoroughly to mix.

Note: Bulghar wheat is also called burghul and cracked wheat.

Desserts

Baked Stuffed Apple with a Cranberry and Orange Sauce

120 g (4 oz) cranberries
juice of 1 orange
5 ml (1 tsp) sugar
2 Bramley apples
10 ml (2 tsp) raisins

1 Put the cranberries in a small saucepan with the orange juice and sugar. Bring to a simmer and cook gently until soft. Allow to cool. Purée in a blender or food processor, then pass through a sieve into a bowl to remove the seeds and skins.

2 Peel the apples, retaining the stalks if possible, then carefully slice off the tops and set aside for the lids. Carefully scoop out the cores, using an apple corer. Cut a thin slice off the bottom of each apple, so they sit flat on a baking tray.

3 Spoon the raisins into the middle of the apples and replace the lids. Bake in a preheated oven at 180°C (350°F) mark 4 for 15-20 minutes, or until the apples are tender but still retaining their shape.

4 Reheat the cranberry and orange sauce. Transfer the baked stuffed apples to warmed serving plates, pour on the sauce and serve at once.

Grilled Bananas with Cardamom Butter and Vanilla Ice Cream

2 bananas (unpeeled)
2 cardamom pods
50 g (2 oz) soft dark brown sugar
50 g (2 oz) butter

Ice Cream:
2 egg yolks
35 g (1¼ oz) vanilla sugar (see note)
100 ml (3½ fl oz) full-cream milk
60 ml (2 fl oz) double cream

To Serve:
icing sugar, for dusting
mint sprigs, to decorate

1 First make the ice cream. Beat the egg yolks and vanilla sugar together until the mixture is very pale – almost white in colour. Meanwhile, gently heat the milk in a heavy-based saucepan.

2 Beat the cream into the egg and sugar mixture, then gradually whisk in the hot milk. Return to the saucepan and cook over a moderate heat, stirring constantly, until thickened enough to coat the back of a wooden spoon; do not allow to boil or the custard will curdle.

3 Turn into a chilled bowl and allow the mixture to cool to room temperature. Transfer to an ice-cream maker and churn for 45 minutes or until frozen.

4 To prepare the bananas, line the grill pan with foil and replace the rack. Make a slit along the length of each banana skin then, at each end, cut across the slits to form a 'T'.

5 Break open the cardamom pods, empty the seeds into a mortar and pound with the pestle. Add half of the sugar and pound to mix with the crushed cardamom seeds.

6 Beat the butter and cardamom mixture together in a bowl. Press the mixture along the length of each banana slit.

7 Lay the bananas, open-side up, on the grill rack. Grill under a preheated high grill for 3-5 minutes, until the banana flesh is softened and the butter melted. Sprinkle the rest of the sugar on top and grill until the topping is caramelised.

8 Serve the bananas piping hot in their skins, dusted with icing sugar and decorated with mint sprigs. Accompany with the vanilla ice cream.

Note: To make vanilla sugar, place a vanilla pod in a jar of caster sugar and leave to infuse.

Steamed Chocolate Pudding, served with a Rich Chocolate Sauce

55 ml (2 fl oz) milk
25 g (1 oz) good-quality plain chocolate
20 g (¾ oz) butter
20 g (¾ oz) caster sugar
1 egg, separated
55 g (2¼ oz) fresh white breadcrumbs
2.5 ml (½ tsp) baking powder

Chocolate Sauce:
55 g (2¼ oz) dark chocolate
10 g (⅓ oz) butter
22 ml (1½ tbsp) water
22 ml (1½ tbsp) brandy

To Decorate:
15 ml (1 tbsp) double cream

1 Grease 2 dariole moulds and line the base of each one with a small disc of greaseproof paper.

2 For the puddings, put the milk in a small heavy-based pan and grate the chocolate into it. Heat gently until the chocolate is melted.

3 Cream the butter and sugar together in a bowl. Beat in the egg yolk, chocolate milk mixture, breadcrumbs and baking powder.

4 In a separate bowl, whisk the egg white until fairly stiff, then fold into the pudding mixture.

5 Spoon into the prepared dariole moulds and cover each with a piece of foil, securing loosely under the rim. Place in a steamer or pan containing a 5 cm (2 inch) depth of boiling water. Steam for approximately 30 minutes.

6 Meanwhile, make the sauce. Put the chocolate, butter and water in a small heavy-based pan. Stir constantly over a gentle heat until melted and smooth. Stir in the brandy and set aside to cool.

7 Leave the puddings in their moulds for 2 minutes, then turn out onto warmed serving plates. Pour the chocolate sauce around the puddings. Dot a little cream onto the sauce and feather with a skewer to decorate. Serve at once.

Chocolate Puddle Pudding

225 g (8 oz) good-quality plain chocolate,
* in pieces*
300 ml (½ pint) milk
30 ml (2 tbsp) brandy
50 g (2 oz) unsalted butter
150 g (5 oz) caster sugar
2 eggs, separated
25 g (1 oz) self-raising flour
25 g (1 oz) cocoa powder

To Serve:
icing sugar or cocoa powder, for dusting
whipped cream (optional)

1 Put the chocolate and milk in a heatproof bowl over a pan of simmering water until melted. Stir until smooth, then add the brandy.

2 Cream the butter and sugar together in a bowl until pale and fluffy. Beat in the egg yolks, one at a time. Sift the flour and cocoa together over the mixture and fold in, using a metal spoon.

3 Add the melted chocolate mixture and fold in until evenly mixed.

4 Whisk the egg whites in another bowl until they just hold their shape. Fold into the chocolate mixture until evenly incorporated.

5 Pour the mixture into buttered 250 ml (8 fl oz) individual soufflé dishes.

6 Stand the soufflé dishes in a roasting tin, containing a 2.5 cm (1 inch) depth of boiling water. Cook in a preheated oven at 180°C (350°F) mark 4 for 20 minutes, until a crust forms on the surface of the puddings. Remove the dishes from the roasting tin.

7 Dust with cocoa powder or icing sugar according to taste and serve at once, with whipped cream if liked.

Note: This pudding is sufficient to serve 3. It should have a mousse-like texture on the outside and a gooey chocolate sauce in the centre.

Baked Camellia Pudding, with a Raspberry Coulis

Sponge Base:
40 g (1½ oz) plain flour
pinch of salt
1 large egg
50 g (2 oz) caster sugar

Ice Cream Filling:
225 g (8 oz) raspberries
dash of crème de cassis
220 g (7½ oz) can condensed milk
150 ml (¼ pint) single cream

Meringue:
2 large egg whites
125 g (4 oz) caster sugar

Raspberry Coulis:
50 g (2 oz) raspberries
icing sugar, to taste

To Decorate:
icing sugar, for dusting
camellia flowers (optional)

1 To make the sponge base, sift the flour and salt onto a sheet of greaseproof paper. Whisk the egg in a large heatproof bowl, then gradually whisk in the sugar. Place the bowl over a pan of simmering water and continue whisking for about 5 minutes, until the mixture is pale, creamy and thick enough to leave a ribbon trail when the whisk is lifted. Take the bowl off the heat, add the flour and fold in, using a metal spoon.

2 Spoon the mixture into a base-lined and greased 20 cm (8 inch) sandwich cake tin. Bake in a preheated oven at 175°C (340°F) mark 3½ for 20-25 minutes until golden and springy to the touch. Turn out and cool on a wire rack.

3 For the filling, put 10 raspberries in a small bowl, add a dash of cassis and set aside to macerate.

4 To make the ice cream, purée the rest of the raspberries in a blender or food processor, then pass through a sieve into a bowl to remove the seeds. Stir in the condensed milk and cream. Transfer to an ice-cream maker and churn for about 20 minutes until firm.

5 Spoon the ice cream into two individual bombe moulds, making a hollow in the middle. Spoon the macerated raspberries into the hollow. Freeze until firm.

6 To make the coulis, purée the raspberries in a blender or food processor and pass through a sieve into a bowl. Sweeten with icing sugar to taste.

7 Cut 2 rounds from the sponge base, the same size as the base of the bombe moulds, sprinkle with a little cassis and set aside.

8 To make the meringue, whisk the egg whites in a bowl until stiff. Gradually whisk in the sugar, a spoonful at a time, to make a stiff, shiny meringue.

9 Place the sponge rounds on a baking sheet. Turn out the ice cream bombes onto the sponge bases, then cover completely with the meringue. Bake in a preheated oven at 220°C (425°F) mark 7 for 3-5 minutes, until the meringue is tinged golden brown.

10 Transfer the meringue bombes to individual serving plates, sprinkle with icing sugar and spread a pool of raspberry coulis around one side. Serve at once, decorated with a camellia if available.

Pear and Calvados Crumble, served with a Crème Anglais

4 William's pears
50 ml (2 fl oz) Calvados
100 g (4 oz) wholemeal flour
50 g (2 oz) butter, in pieces
25 g (1 oz) caster sugar

Crème Anglais:
3 egg yolks
60 g (2¼ oz) caster sugar
250 ml (8 fl oz) milk
4 drops of vanilla essence

1 Dice the pears, discarding the cores, but do not peel them.

2 Place the pears in a heavy-based saucepan and heat gently until they start to soften. Add the Calvados and carefully flame. When the flame has died down, transfer the pears to an ovenproof dish.

3 To make the crumble topping, sift the flour into a bowl and rub in the butter until the mixture resembles breadcrumbs. Stir in the sugar. Spread the crumble on top of the pears and bake in a preheated oven at 180°C (350°F) mark 4 for 20-25 minutes.

4 Meanwhile, make the crème anglais. Put the egg yolks and 15 g (½ oz) of the sugar in a bowl and whisk until the mixture is thick and mousse-like. Meanwhile, put the milk, remaining sugar and vanilla essence in a heavy-based saucepan and bring to the boil. Pour the hot milk onto the egg mixture, whisking constantly. Return the mixture to the pan and cook over a low heat, stirring continuously with a wooden spoon, until thickened enough the coat the back of the spoon; do not allow to boil.

5 Serve the pear crumble hot, with the crème anglais.

Note: If preferred the crème anglais can be prepared ahead and refrigerated before serving chilled – with the hot crumble.

Bramley Apple Soufflé with Calvados Cream and Caramelised Apple

4 Bramley apples
juice of 1 lemon
75 g (3 oz) caster sugar
150 ml (¼ pint) water
dash of Calvados
5 ml (1 tsp) cornflour, blended with 10 ml
   (2 tsp) water
2 egg whites
large knob of butter, softened

Calvados Cream:
300 ml (½ pint) double cream
25 g (1 oz) caster sugar
1 vanilla pod, split, seeds extracted
dash of Calvados

To Decorate:
icing sugar, for dusting

1 Carefully scoop out the insides from three of the apples, (through the tops), leaving a 1 cm (½ inch) shell intact on the apple skins; reserve the scooped-out flesh and cores. Immerse the apple 'shells' in a bowl of chilled water acidulated with the lemon juice.

2 Slice the remaining apple finely, discarding the core. Spread out the apple slices on a baking tray and sprinkle with a little sugar. Cook in a preheated oven at 220°C (425°F) mark 7 for 20 minutes, or until caramelised, sprinkling with a little more sugar if necessary. Allow to cool.

3 In the meantime, put the reserved apple flesh and cores in a saucepan with 100 ml (3½ fl oz) water and 25 g (1 oz) sugar. Bring to the boil, then remove from the heat. Purée in a blender or food processor, then pass through a chinois or fine sieve.

4 Dissolve 25 g (1 oz) sugar in 50 ml (2 fl oz) water in a clean saucepan, then add the puréed apple. Stir in a dash of Calvados and the blended cornflour. Cook, stirring constantly, until thickened and smooth. Turn into a chilled bowl to cool.

5 To make the calvados cream, in a bowl whip the cream with the sugar and vanilla seeds until thick. Flavour with a dash of Calvados to taste, cover and set aside.

6 Whisk the egg whites in a bowl until they form stiff peaks. Whisk in 15 ml (1 tbsp) sugar, then fold into the cooled apple mixture.

7 Drain the apple 'shells', butter the insides generously, then sprinkle with sugar. Chill in the freezer for a few minutes until the butter is hardened.

8 Spoon the soufflé mixture into the apple shells, place on a baking tray and cook in a preheated oven at 180°C (350°F) mark 4 for 10-15 minutes.

9 Meanwhile, layer the caramelised apple slices and calvados cream on one side of each serving plate to form 'stacks'. Place the cooked soufflés next to the apple stacks, dust lightly with icing sugar and serve at once.

Note: This recipe serves 3.

Fresh Fruit Fettucini with a Summer Fruit Medley and Cassis Coulis

Fettucini:

100 g (3½ oz) Italian pasta flour "type 00"
10 g (½ oz) semolina
½ medium egg, beaten
10 ml (2 tsp) oil
20-30 ml (4-6 tsp) warm summer fruit cordial, or blackcurrant cordial

Cassis Coulis:

100 g (3½ oz) sugar
125 ml (4 fl oz) water
150 g (5 oz) raspberries
150 g (5 oz) strawberries
100 ml (3½ fl oz) crème de cassis

To Serve:

clotted cream

1 To make the pasta, mix together the pasta flour and semolina in a mound on a clean work surface. Make a well in the centre and add the egg, oil and warm fruit cordial. Stir the liquid ingredients into the flour with a fork to begin with, then use your fingers to mix the ingredients together. Knead to a very firm smooth dough, then wrap in cling film and leave to rest in a cool place for 30 minutes.

2 Using a pasta machine, roll out the pasta to the required thickness, passing the dough through the machine repeatedly and narrowing the setting by one notch each time, until you obtain the required thickness.

3 Fit the tagliatelle cutters and pass the pasta through to cut into noodles. Hang over a pasta dryer or lay on clean tea-towels and leave to dry slightly for about 10 minutes before cooking.

4 To make the coulis, dissolve the sugar in the water in a heavy-based pan over a low heat, then increase the heat and boil until the syrup registers 150°C (300°F) on a sugar thermometer. Add the raspberries, strawberries and cassis. Strain the syrup, reserving the fruit, then pass the coulis through a muslin-lined sieve.

5 Bring a large pan of water to the boil. Add the pasta and cook for 2-3 minutes until *al dente*, tender but firm to the bite.

6 Meanwhile, warm the fruit in a small amount of the coulis.

7 Drain the pasta thoroughly and divide between warmed serving plates. Spoon the warm fruits on top and surround with the coulis. Serve at once, with clotted cream.

Hot Raspberry Soufflé with a Warm Raspberry Coulis

250 ml (8 fl oz) milk
225 g (8 oz) caster sugar, plus extra for
  sprinkling
3 egg yolks
25 g (1 oz) plain flour
15 g (½ oz) butter
500 g (1 lb 2 oz) raspberries
30 ml (2 tbsp) framboise liqueur
500 ml (16 fl oz) water
squeeze of lemon juice, to taste
5 egg whites
6 macaroons, crushed
icing sugar, for dusting

1 Butter 3 ramekins and sprinkle with sugar to coat the base and sides; place in the refrigerator.

2 Put the milk in a heavy-based saucepan with 40 g (1½oz) sugar and slowly bring to the boil.

3 Meanwhile, whisk the egg yolks and 25 g (1 oz) of the sugar together in a bowl for about 5 minutes until pale and thick. Add the flour and beat until the mixture is very smooth, then gradually pour on the hot milk, whisking all the time.

4 Return the mixture to the saucepan and place over a moderate heat. Bring to the boil, whisking constantly, and cook for about 3 minutes until the pastry cream has lost any taste of flour. Remove from the heat and flake the butter over the surface; keep warm.

5 Place 9 raspberries in a bowl, sprinkle with 15 ml (1 tbsp) framboise and set aside to macerate.

6 Put the rest of the raspberries into a saucepan with 150 g (5 oz) sugar and the water. Bring to a simmer and cook gently for 5 minutes. Let cool slightly, then purée in a blender or food processor and pass through a sieve into a measuring jug to remove the pips.

7 Return two thirds of the raspberry purée to the pan and bring to the boil over a high heat. Let bubble until reduced to a thick jam consistency. Let cool, then fold into the pastry cream. Transfer to a bowl.

8 Meanwhile, add the remaining 15 ml (1 tbsp) framboise to the reserved raspberry purée and sharpen with lemon juice to taste, to make the coulis. Keep warm in a bain-marie.

9 Whisk the egg whites in a bowl until they form soft peaks, then add the remaining 15 g (½ oz) sugar and whisk to a soft, white meringue. Stir a third of the egg whites into the pastry cream mixture to lighten it, then carefully fold in the rest, using a large metal spoon.

10 Half-fill the prepared ramekins with the soufflé mixture, then place 3 macerated raspberries and 2 crushed macaroons on top of each. Cover with the remaining soufflé mixture and smooth the surface.

11 Run a knife around the edge of each ramekin and bake in a preheated oven at 230°C (450°F) mark 8 for 8-10 minutes. Meanwhile, transfer the raspberry coulis to a warmed serving jug. On removing from the oven, dust the hot soufflés with icing sugar and serve immediately, accompanied by the raspberry coulis.

Note: This recipe serves 3.

Autumn Fruit Tarte Tatin with Blackberry Ice Cream

Pastry:
75 g (3 oz) plain flour
50 g (2 oz) butter
7.5 ml (½ tbsp) caster sugar
1 small egg yolk
finely grated zest of 1 lemon

Filling:
25 g (1 oz) butter
30 ml (2 tbsp) light brown sugar
1 dessert apple
1 plum

Ice Cream:
200 g (7 oz) blackberries
15 ml (1 tbsp) lemon juice
175 ml (6 fl oz) full-fat milk
1 egg yolk
70 g (2¾ oz) caster sugar
60 ml (2 fl oz) double cream

1 First make the ice cream. Purée the blackberries together with the lemon juice and milk in a food processor or blender, then pass through a sieve into a bowl to remove the pips.

2 Beat the egg yolk and sugar together in a bowl until pale and creamy. In another bowl, whip the cream until thick. Fold the blackberry purée into the egg yolk mixture, then fold in the cream.

3 Transfer to an ice-cream maker and churn for 25-40 minutes until frozen.

4 To make the pastry, put the flour, butter, sugar, egg yolk and lemon zest in a food processor and process just until the dough forms a ball. Gather the dough, wrap in cling film and leave to rest in the refrigerator for 20 minutes.

5 Meanwhile, butter two shallow 10 cm (4 inch) individual flan tins, then line with rounds of non-stick baking parchment to overlap the edge of each tin by 2.5 cm (1 inch). Spread 15 g (½ oz) butter over the surface of each paper round and sprinkle the brown sugar evenly on top.

6 Peel, core and slice the apple and arrange the apple slices around the edge of the tins (on the paper). Halve and stone the plum, trim to the same depth as the apple slices and place one half, skin-side down, in the centre of each tin.

7 Halve the pastry and roll out each piece to a round, the same size as the tins. Lift the pastry rounds on top of the fruit and prick with a fork. Cover with foil and bake in the centre of a preheated oven at 200°C (400°F) mark 6 for 20 minutes. Remove the foil and bake for a further 10 minutes.

8 Lift the tarts out of the tins, using the paper, and invert onto individual plates, so the fruit is uppermost. Serve warm, with scoops of the blackberry ice cream.

Chocolate and Walnut Tart, with a Rhubarb and Raspberry Compote and Orange Liqueur Cream

75 g (3 oz) quality plain chocolate
25 g (1 oz) butter, diced
30 ml (2 tbsp) whipping cream
4 eggs, separated
30 ml (2 tbsp) caster sugar
25 g (1 oz) plain flour
15 ml (1 tbsp) cocoa powder
50 g (2 oz) walnuts, toasted and roughly
  chopped

Fruit Compote:
2 rhubarb stalks, trimmed and cut into
  short lengths
15-30 ml (1-2 tbsp) sugar
30 ml (2 tbsp) water
125 g (4 oz) raspberries
dash of Grand Marnier
squeeze of lemon juice

Orange Liqueur Cream:
60 ml (4 tbsp) whipping cream
dash of Grand Marnier
a little icing sugar, to taste

To Decorate:
icing sugar, for dusting

1 Butter a 15 cm (6 inch) round cake tin and dust with flour. Melt the chocolate in a heatproof bowl over a pan of simmering water. Stir in the butter, followed by the cream, until smooth. Take off the heat.

2 Whisk the egg whites in a bowl until they form soft peaks. Fold in the sugar, a spoonful at a time. Fold in 3 egg yolks.

3 Sift the flour and cocoa powder together over the mixture and fold in, then fold in the chocolate and butter mixture.

4 Spoon half of the mixture into the prepared tin and spread evenly. Sprinkle the nuts over the surface, then cover with the rest of the chocolate mixture. Bake in a preheated oven at 180°C (350°F) mark 4 for 25-30 minutes. Allow to cool.

5 To make the fruit compote, put the rhubarb in a heavy-based pan with the sugar and water. Cover and cook over a low heat for 5 minutes or until the rhubarb is just tender. Add the raspberries and cook for 1 minute. Turn into a bowl, add the Grand Marnier and lemon juice and set aside to cool.

6 For the orange liqueur cream, whip the cream in a bowl until thick and flavour with the Grand Marnier and icing sugar to taste.

7 To serve, carefully remove the chocolate tart from the tin and cut into portions. Place a portion on each serving plate and dust with icing sugar. Serve accompanied by the fruit compote and flavoured cream.

Lemon Tart with a Raspberry Coulis

Pastry:

75 g (3 oz) plain flour
50 g (2 oz) butter, in pieces
25 g (1 oz) icing sugar
1 egg yolk

Filling:

100 g (4 oz) caster sugar
finely grated zest and juice of 1 lemon
1 egg
1 egg yolk
50 g (2 oz) unsalted butter

Raspberry Coulis:

125 g (4 oz) raspberries
50 g (2 oz) icing sugar, or to taste

1 Put the flour and butter in a food processor and process briefly until the mixture resembles fine breadcrumbs. Add the icing sugar and egg yolk and process just until the dough holds together in a ball. If time, wrap in cling film and leave to rest in the refrigerator for 20 minutes.

2 Press the pastry directly into two individual 11 cm (4½ inch) flan tins to line the base and sides. Line with greaseproof paper and baking beans and blind bake in a preheated oven at 180°C (350°F) mark 4 for 20 minutes. Remove from the oven and take out the greaseproof paper and beans. Increase the oven temperature to 200°C (400°F) mark 6.

3 Meanwhile, make the filling. Put the sugar, lemon zest and juice in a small heavy-based saucepan over a low heat until dissolved. Take off the heat.

4 Beat the whole egg and egg yolk together in a bowl and add to the lemon syrup with half of the butter. Return to a very low heat and cook gently, stirring all the time, until the mixture begins to thicken; do not allow to boil or it will curdle. Add the remaining butter and cook, stirring, until thickened.

5 Take off the heat and divide the filling between the flan cases. Bake in the oven at 200°C (400°F) mark 6 for 15 minutes. Leave to stand for 5-10 minutes.

6 Meanwhile, to make the raspberry coulis, purée the raspberries in a blender or food processor, then pass through a sieve into a bowl to remove the pips. Sweeten with the icing sugar, to taste.

7 To serve, transfer each warm lemon flan to a serving plate and surround with raspberry coulis.

Mango Tarte Tatin

Pâte Sucrée:
100 g (3½ oz) plain flour
pinch of salt
50 g (2 oz) butter (at room temperature)
2 egg yolks
50 g (2 oz) caster sugar

Filling:
100 g (3½ oz) demerara sugar
100 g (3½ oz) butter
10 ml (2 tsp) water
1 medium mango, halved, stoned and peeled

To Serve:
crème fraîche
pinch of ground cinnamon, to taste
  (optional)

1 To make the pâte sucrée, sift the flour and salt onto a clean work surface, make a well in the centre and add the butter, egg yolks and sugar. Using the fingertips, pinch and work the sugar, butter and egg yolks together until well blended. Gradually work in the flour.

2 Knead the dough lightly until smooth. Wrap in cling film and leave to rest in the refrigerator for at least 30 minutes.

3 Roll out the pastry on a lightly floured surface to a 5 mm (¼ inch) thickness.

4 For the filling, divide the demerara sugar, butter and water between two heatproof small, shallow glass bowls, measuring about 10 cm (4 inches) across.

5 Place a mango half in each bowl, rounded-side down, and cut 2 pastry rounds large enough to cover the bowls. Position the pastry rounds over the bowls. Cook in a preheated oven at 200°C (400°F) mark 6 for 10-15 minutes or until the pastry is crisp.

6 Invert the tarte tatins onto warmed serving plates. Serve with crème fraîche, flavoured with a little ground cinnamon if desired.

Note: Make sure you remove the tough outer layer of flesh from the mango by peeling it twice.

Blueberry Mango Tartlet with Strawberry Sauce

Pastry:
60 g (2 oz) butter
100 g (3½ oz) plain flour
15 g (½ oz) ground almonds
40 g (1½ oz) icing sugar
1 egg

Filling:
100 g (3½ oz) mascarpone
finely grated zest and juice of ½ lime
icing sugar, to taste
½ mango, peeled and finely chopped

Strawberry Sauce:
125 g (4 oz) strawberries
15 ml (1 tbsp) icing sugar
5 ml (1 tsp) Grand Marnier

To Finish:
50-75 g (2-3 oz) blueberries
icing sugar, for dusting
½ mango, peeled and sliced
mint sprigs, to decorate

1 To make the pastry, put all of the ingredients in a food processor and process, using the pulse button, until a ball of dough is formed. Wrap in cling film and leave to rest in the refrigerator for 1 hour.

2 Roll out the pastry thinly on a lightly floured surface and use to line two individual 10 cm (4 inch) flan tins. Line with greaseproof paper and baking beans and bake blind in a preheated oven at 190°C (375°F) mark 5 for 15 minutes. Remove the paper and beans. Return the pastry cases to the oven and bake for a further 5 minutes until the bases are firm and the pastry is pale golden. Allow to cool.

3 For the filling, in a bowl, mix the mascarpone with the lime zest and juice; sweeten with icing sugar to taste. Fold in the chopped mango.

4 To make the strawberry sauce, put all of the ingredients in a food processor or blender and work to a purée. Pass through a nylon sieve into a bowl.

5 To serve, spoon the mango filling into the pastry cases and top with the blueberries. Place on individual serving plates and surround with the strawberry sauce. Decorate with the mango slices and mint sprigs.

Shortbread Tartlet filled with Rich Chocolate Mousse, served with Coffee and Almond Creams

Shortbread:
120 g (4 oz) salted butter
75 g (3 oz) caster sugar
150 g (5 oz) plain flour
25 g (1 oz) rice flour

Chocolate Mousse:
70 g (2¾ oz) butter
30 g (1¼ oz) cocoa powder
135 ml (4½ fl oz) double cream
15 g (½ oz) icing sugar
30 g (1¼ oz) plain dark chocolate
2 egg yolks
65 g (2½ oz) caster sugar

Almond Cream:
60 ml (4 tbsp) double cream
5 ml (1 tsp) icing sugar, or to taste
2-3 drops of almond essence

Coffee Cream:
25 g (1 oz) milk chocolate
60 ml (4 tbsp) double cream
  (approximately)
5 ml (1 tsp) coffee essence

To Decorate:
redcurrants and/or strawberries

1 To make the shortbread, cream the butter and sugar together until pale and fluffy. Sift in the flours and stir into the creamed mixture, using a wooden spoon. Gather up the dough, knead lightly, then wrap in cling film and leave to rest in the refrigerator for 20 minutes.

2 To make the chocolate mousse, melt the butter in a pan, stir in the cocoa until evenly blended; let cool slightly. Whip the cream and icing sugar together in a bowl, until thick enough to leave a ribbon trail when the whisk is lifted; set aside. Melt the chocolate in a bowl over a pan of simmering water; let cool slightly.

3 Whisk the egg yolks and sugar together in a bowl until thick and mousse-like, then whisk in the melted chocolate, and butter and cocoa mixture. Fold the whipped cream into the mousse. Cover and chill in the refrigerator until set.

4 Roll out the shortbread dough thinly on a lightly floured surface and use to line two 7.5 cm (3 inch) tartlet tins. Bake in a preheated oven at 180°C (350°F) mark 4 for about 10 minutes, until pale golden.

5 For the almond cream, flavour the cream with icing sugar and almond essence to taste, mixing with a fork.

6 To prepare the coffee cream, melt the chocolate in a bowl over a pan of simmering water. Stir until smooth, then take off the heat and let cool a little. While still warm, stir in the cream, then mix in the coffee essence, using a fork. If the sauce becomes too thick as it cools, thin with a little more cream.

7 To serve, put the chocolate mousse into a piping bag fitted with a fluted nozzle and pipe into the shortbread tartlets. Spread a pool of coffee cream around one side of each serving plate, and a pool of almond cream around the other side. Position a chocolate tartlet in the centre and decorate with fruit.

Ginger and Apricot Baked Alaska, with an Orange and Apricot Coulis

2 slices rich, dark ginger cake, each 2 cm
  (¾ inch) thick (see right)
30 ml (2 tbsp) rum
1 eating apple
6 dried apricots, chopped
60 ml (4 tbsp) orange juice
15 g (½ oz/1 tbsp) flaked almonds
2 egg whites
100 g (3½ oz) caster sugar
2 scoops or slices of rich dairy vanilla ice
  cream

Coulis:
125 g (4 oz) fresh apricots
30-45 ml (2-3 tbsp) orange juice
a little sugar, to taste

1 Place each slice of ginger cake on an ovenproof plate and sprinkle with the rum.

2 Quarter, core and slice the apple into a small saucepan. Add the chopped dried apricots and orange juice. Simmer gently for about 5 minutes or until tender. Add the flaked almonds to the fruit and spoon over the soaked cake.

3 To make the coulis, put the apricots into a small heavy-based pan with the orange juice and poach gently until tender. Let cool slightly, then purée in a blender or food processor and sweeten with sugar to taste. Pass through a sieve into a bowl; set aside.

4 Whisk the egg whites in a bowl until very stiff and dry, then whisk in the sugar a little at a time, making sure the meringue is stiff before each addition of sugar.

5 When ready to serve, place a scoop or slice of vanilla ice cream on each portion of fruit and pipe or spread the meringue over the fruit, ice cream and cake, making sure it is completely covered. Bake in a preheated oven at 200°C (400°F) mark 6 for 4-5 minutes until golden brown. Surround with the orange and apricot coulis, and serve immediately.

Ginger Cake

125 g (5 oz) butter
100 g (4 oz) soft brown sugar
30 ml (2 tbsp) black treacle
15 ml (1 tbsp) water
200 g (7 oz) self-raising flour
2.5 ml (½ tsp) ground mixed spice
10 ml (2 tsp) finely chopped fresh root ginger
2 large eggs, lightly beaten

1 Put the butter, sugar, black treacle and water in a heavy-based pan over a gentle heat until the fat is melted and the sugar dissolved. Remove from the heat and let cool for 10 minutes.

2 Sift the flour, spice and ginger into a bowl. Pour in the melted mixture and eggs; beat thoroughly.

3 Turn the mixture into a greased 18 cm (7 inch) square tin and bake in a preheated oven at 180°C (350°F) mark 4 for 45 minutes. Leave in the tin for 2-3 minutes, then turn out on to a wire rack to cool completely.

4 When cold, store in an airtight tin; this cake improves if kept for a day before slicing.

Lemon Meringue Roulade

4 egg whites
175 g (6 oz) caster sugar
5 ml (1 tsp) ground cinnamon
15 ml (1 tbsp) flaked almonds
300 ml (½ pint) double cream
150 ml (¼ pint) homemade lemon curd
  (see right)
icing sugar, for dusting (optional)

1 Line a 33 x 23 cm (13 x 9 inch) Swiss roll tin with non-stick baking parchment.

2 Whisk the egg whites in a bowl until very stiff. Gradually beat in 150 g (5 oz) of the caster sugar.

3 Spoon the mixture into the prepared tin, spreading it evenly to the edges and into the corners.

4 Mix together the remaining sugar, cinnamon and flaked almonds. Sprinkle evenly over the top of the meringue. Bake in a preheated oven at 180°C (350°F) mark 4 for 15 minutes.

6 Leave in the tin until cool, then turn out the roulade on to a clean tea-towel. Carefully peel off the lining paper.

7 Whip the cream in a bowl until it forms soft peaks, then fold in the lemon curd.

8 Spread the lemon cream over the roulade and roll it up from one of the shorter sides, using the tea-towel to push the roulade along.

9 Dust with a little icing sugar to serve, if desired.

Homemade Lemon Curd

110 g (4 oz) unsalted butter
finely grated zest and juice of 3 lemons
225 g (8 oz) granulated sugar
3 eggs
1 egg yolk

1 Melt the butter slowly in a glass bowl or jug in the microwave.

2 Add the lemon zest and juice, the sugar, whole eggs and extra egg yolk. Mix thoroughly.

3 Return to the microwave and cook on HIGH for 2 minutes. Stir thoroughly.

4 Cook for a further 3-4 minutes, stirring every minute until the lemon curd is thickened and creamy; do not overcook or it will be too firm. Allow to cool; use as required.

Note: If preferred, the lemon curd can be cooked in a bain-marie, or heatproof bowl over a pan of simmering water; it must be stirred during cooking.

Toffee Pecan Nut Cheesecake with Butterscotch Sauce

Base:
25 g (1 oz) pecan nuts
50 g (2 oz) gingernut biscuits
25 g (1 oz) butter, melted

Filling:
1 ripe banana, roughly chopped
1 egg
7.5 ml (1½ tsp) lemon juice
100 g (4 oz) full-fat curd cheese
100 g (4 oz) fromage frais
50 g (2 oz) caster sugar

Sauce:
25 g (1 oz) butter
25 g (1 oz) brown sugar
50 g (2 oz) golden syrup
75 g (3 oz) double cream
few drops of vanilla essence
few chopped pecan nuts, chopped

To Decorate:
few pecan nuts

1 To make the base, crush the pecan nuts and biscuits in a food processor, then add to the melted butter and mix well. Divide between 2-3 lightly greased 7.5 cm (3 inch) metal rings placed on a baking sheet. Bake in a preheated oven at 150°C (300°F) mark 2 for 10 minutes. Let cool.

2 To make the filling, put all of the ingredients in the food processor and process until smooth and evenly blended; do not over-mix.

3 Pour the filling over the biscuit base and bake in the oven for 20 minutes. Leave to cool in the oven with the door slightly ajar for 10-15 minutes.

4 Meanwhile, make the sauce. Put the butter, sugar and syrup in a heavy-based saucepan over a low heat until melted and smooth. Just before serving, stir in the cream, vanilla essence and chopped nuts; do not allow to boil or it will curdle.

5 Run a knife around the edge of each warm cheesecake and carefully place on individual serving plates. Decorate with pecan nuts and serve warm, with the butterscotch sauce to one side.

Mascarpone and Fromage Frais Cheesecake, served with a Raspberry Coulis

Base:
85 g (3 oz) Digestive biscuits
25 g (1 oz) butter
pinch of ground cinnamon

Filling:
170 g (6 oz) mascarpone
170 g (6 oz) fromage frais
2 eggs
15 ml (1 tbsp) caster sugar
few drops of vanilla essence

Coulis:
350 g (12 oz) raspberries
sugar, to taste

To Finish:
icing sugar, for dusting

1 Crush the biscuits in a food processor. Melt the butter in the microwave or in a small pan over a low heat. Mix the biscuits, ground cinnamon and butter together well. Divide between two deep 7.5 cm (3 inch) individual fluted flan tins and press onto the bases, in an even layer.

2 To make the filling, combine the mascarpone, fromage frais, eggs, sugar and vanilla essence together in a bowl. Beat until smooth and creamy.

3 Pour the mixture on top of the biscuit bases. Bake in a preheated oven at 150°C (300°F) mark 2 for 30 minutes, or until golden and firm at the edges (see note).

4 In the meantime, prepare the coulis. Set aside a few raspberries for decoration. Put the rest in a blender or food processor and work to a purée. Pass through a nylon sieve into a bowl, to get rid of the seeds, then add sugar to taste.

5 Allow the cheesecakes to cool before serving.

6 To serve, carefully unmould the cheesecakes and place on individual serving plates. Decorate with the reserved raspberries and a sprinkling of icing sugar. Surround with the raspberry coulis.

Note: When cooked the cheesecake should be firm around the edges with a golden crust, but still a little runny in the middle; it firms up on cooling.

Mango Meringue Chinchilla with Coconut and Chilli Ice Cream

Meringue Chinchilla:
1 mango, halved, peeled and stoned
3 medium eggs, separated
75 g (3 oz) caster sugar
25 g (1 oz) plain flour
20 g (¾ oz) ground almonds

Ice Cream:
100 ml (3½ fl oz) canned coconut milk
30 ml (3 tbsp) double cream
75 ml (5 tbsp) single cream
few drops of Malibu
1-2 hot red chillies, to taste
2 egg yolks
50 g (2 oz) caster sugar
25-40 g (1-1½ oz) shredded coconut

To Serve:
icing sugar, for dusting

1 First make the ice cream. Put the coconut milk, both creams, Malibu and chillies in a heatproof bowl over a pan of simmering water and heat gently until lukewarm. Set aside to infuse for 20-30 minutes, then remove the chillies.

2 Whisk the egg yolks and sugar together in a heatproof bowl until thick and creamy. Add the shredded coconut, then pour in the infused cream mixture, whisking all the time. Stand the bowl over a pan of simmering water and stir constantly until the custard is thick enough to lightly coat the back of the wooden spoon.

3 Pour into a chilled bowl and allow to cool, then transfer to an ice-cream maker and churn until frozen.

4 In the meantime, make the meringue chinchilla. Finely dice half of the mango flesh, cover and set aside; purée the rest of the mango in a blender or food processor and pass through a sieve into a bowl.

5 Whisk two of the egg whites in a bowl until stiff. Whisk in 50 g (2 oz) of the sugar, a spoonful at a time, to make a stiff, shiny meringue.

6 Spread 10-15 ml (2-3 tsp) of the mango pulp in the bottom of each of 2 ramekins and top with the meringue.

7 Whisk 2 egg yolks with the remaining egg white and sugar in a clean bowl until very creamy and frothy. Sift in the flour, add the ground almonds and fold in gently. Add the remaining mango pulp and diced mango flesh and fold in until evenly incorporated. Spoon the mixture on top of the meringue.

8 Run a knife around the edge of the mixture to encourage it to rise during baking. Stand the ramekins in a small roasting tin containing enough boiling water to come halfway up the sides of the dishes. Cook in a preheated oven at 180°C (350°F) mark 4 for 30 minutes until well risen.

9 Dust with icing sugar and serve, accompanied by scoops of the ice cream.

Poached Pear with Butterscotch Sauce

2 pears

Stock Syrup:
900 ml (1½ pints) water
450 g (1 lb) sugar
1 vanilla pod
1 cinnamon stick
1 lemon, halved
1 orange, halved

Butterscotch Sauce:
50 g (2 oz) butter
50 g (2 oz) caster sugar
75 g (3 oz) demerara sugar
125 g (4 oz) golden syrup
120 ml (4 fl oz) double cream

To Decorate:
whipped cream
mint sprigs

1 First make the stock syrup. Put the water and sugar in a saucepan and dissolve over a low heat, then bring to the boil. Add the vanilla pod, cinnamon stick, lemon and orange. Simmer for 1 minute.

2 Peel the pears and scoop out the cores through the base, using an apple corer. Add them to the stock syrup and simmer for about 15-20 minutes, until tender, depending on ripeness. Remove the pears from the pan and leave to cool.

3 To make the butterscotch sauce, melt the butter in a heavy-based pan over a low heat. Add the caster sugar, demerara sugar and golden syrup and stir until dissolved and evenly blended. Bring to the boil, then add the cream and cook, stirring, for 2-3 minutes. Remove from the heat and leave to cool.

4 To serve, place a pear in the middle of each serving plate. Pipe 3 cream whirls around each pear, then spoon the butterscotch sauce onto the plate around the cream and pears. Serve at once, decorated with mint sprigs.

Poached Citrus Pears

2 William's pears
4 oranges
50 ml (2 fl oz) white wine
200 ml (7 fl oz) good-quality orange juice
60 g (2 oz) brown sugar, plus extra for
   coating
12 strawberries, diced

1 Peel the pears, but leave the stalks on. Using an apple corer, carefully scoop out the cores from the base of the pears.

2 Using a zester, remove strips of zest from the oranges. Blanch in boiling water for 10 seconds, drain and set aside for decoration.

3 Put the wine and orange juice in a saucepan and bring to the boil. Peel the oranges, chop the flesh and add to the pan.

4 Add the pears to the poaching liquid and bring to a simmer. Cook for about 10-15 minutes until tender, depending on ripeness. Remove from the pan with a slotted spoon and set aside.

5 Strain the poaching liquid into a clean pan and add the brown sugar. Bring to the boil and reduce by two thirds.

6 Just before serving, roll the pears in brown sugar to coat evenly. Place under a very hot grill and turn frequently to caramelise them. (Alternatively, use a blow torch to do so.)

7 Place a pear in the middle of each warmed serving plate and drizzle the sauce around. Serve at once, decorated with the diced strawberries and orange zest.

Wild Berries with Grand Marnier Cream and Shortbread

25 g (1 oz) blackberries
25 g (1 oz) redcurrants
50 g (2 oz) strawberries
25 g (1 oz) raspberries
30 ml (2 tbsp) Grand Marnier
15 ml (1 tbsp) thin honey

Shortbread:
50 g (2 oz) salted butter
50 g (2 oz) caster sugar
2 drops of vanilla essence
50 g (2 oz) plain flour
50 g (2 oz) farola or rice flour

Grand Marnier Cream:
150 ml (¼ pint) double cream
40 g (1½ oz) caster sugar
15 ml (1 tbsp) yogurt
30 ml (2 tbsp) Grand Marnier

To Finish:
cocoa powder, for dusting
mint sprigs, to decorate

1 Place the soft fruits in a bowl and sprinkle with the Grand Marnier; set aside.

2 To make the shortbread, cream the butter and sugar together until pale and fluffy. Add the vanilla essence, then sift in the flour and farola or rice flour. Stir into the creamed mixture, using a wooden spoon. Gather up the dough, knead lightly, wrap in cling film and leave to rest in the refrigerator for 20 minutes.

3 Meanwhile, lightly whip the cream with the sugar in a bowl until soft peaks form, then fold in the yogurt and Grand Marnier. Cover and chill until needed.

4 Roll out the shortbread dough thinly on a lightly floured surface and cut out ovals or other shapes, using a suitable cutter. Transfer to a baking sheet and bake in a preheated oven at 170°C (325°F) mark 3 for about 10 minutes, until pale golden. Leave on the baking sheet for about 5 minutes, then transfer to a wire rack to cool.

5 Add the honey to the berries and stir gently to mix.

6 To assemble, divide the fruit between individual serving bowls. Spoon the Grand Marnier cream over the fruit and top with the shortbread. Dust with cocoa powder and decorate with mint sprigs.

Blackberries under a blanket of Lemon Syllabub

125 g (4 oz) blackberries
grated zest and juice of 2 lemons
40 g (1½ oz) caster sugar
25 ml (1 fl oz) Grand Marnier
150 ml (¼ pint) double cream

To Decorate:
few blackberries
mint sprigs

To Serve:
Langue de Chat (see right)

1 Divide the blackberries between two stemmed serving glasses.

2 Put the lemon zest and juice, sugar and Grand Marnier in a small pan and stir over a low heat until the sugar is dissolved; let cool.

3 Whip the cream in a bowl until it forms soft peaks. Gradually stir in the lemon syrup until evenly incorporated.

4 Spoon this syllabub over the blackberries and chill in the refrigerator until ready to serve. Decorate with extra blackberries and sprigs of mint. Serve with the langue de chat biscuits.

Langue de Chat

50 g (2 oz) butter
50 g (2 oz) caster sugar
50 g (2 oz) plain flour
1 large egg white
finely grated zest of 1 lemon

1 Beat the butter and sugar together in a bowl until pale and fluffy. Sift the flour over the mixture and stir in.

2 Whisk the egg white in another bowl until stiff, then fold into the creamed mixture, using a metal spoon. Add the lemon zest and mix well.

3 Using a piping bag fitted with a small plain nozzle, pipe 5 cm (2 inch) lengths onto a greased and floured baking tray, spacing them well apart. Bake in a preheated oven at 180°C (350°F) mark 4 for 10 minutes, or until golden brown at the edges.

4 Leave the biscuits on the baking sheet for 1-2 minutes, then transfer to a wire rack to cool.

Note: This quantity makes approximately 20 biscuits. Store in an airtight tin and use as required.

Passion Fruit Delight with Fragrant Cream

Pastry:
125 g (4 oz) unsalted butter
75 g (3 oz) caster sugar
1 egg, beaten
125 g (4 oz) self-raising flour
30 ml (2 tbsp) custard powder

Filling:
3 passion fruit, halved
20 ml (1¼ tbsp) custard powder
15 ml (1 tbsp) caster sugar
150 ml (¼ pint) milk
15 g (½ oz) butter

To Serve:
60 ml (4 tbsp) double cream, whipped
few drops of vanilla essence
icing sugar, for dusting
mint sprigs, to decorate

1 To make the pastry, cream the butter and sugar together in a bowl until light and fluffy. Gradually beat in the egg. Sift the flour and custard powder together over the mixture, then stir in until evenly combined and the mixture is quite stiff. Turn out onto a floured surface and knead for a minute or two until smooth. Wrap in cling film and leave to rest in the refrigerator for 1 hour if possible.

2 To make the filling, scoop the flesh and seeds from two of the passion fruit into a sieve over a bowl and press to extract the juice; discard the contents of the sieve. Add the flesh (including the seeds) from the third passion fruit to the extracted juice; set aside.

3 Mix the custard powder and sugar together in a heatproof glass jug and gradually stir in the milk. Microwave on MEDIUM for 1 minute, stir vigorously, then cook again on MEDIUM for 1-2 minutes until thick. Stir again to ensure there are no lumps, then add the butter and passion fruit. Leave to cool.

4 Line a baking sheet with non-stick baking parchment. Grease and line two 7.5 cm (3 inch) metal rings, allowing the paper to extend 2.5 cm (1 inch) above the rims. Place on the lined baking sheet.

5 Using floured hands, press a thin, even layer of pastry onto the bottom and sides of each ring, to form a flan case, taking care to ensure there are no cracks. Spoon in the passion fruit custard to 5 mm (¼ inch) from the rim of the pastry.

6 On a floured surface, press out 2 thin pastry discs, the same size as the rings and place on top of the filling to form lids. Press the edges of the pastry together to seal. Bake in a preheated oven at 180°C (350°F) mark 4 for 15-20 minutes until lightly golden and risen.

7 Whip the cream in a bowl until soft peaks form, then flavour with 1 or 2 drops of vanilla essence to taste. Chill in the refrigerator until ready to serve.

8 To serve, allow the pies to cool slightly in the rings, then, while still warm, unmould and transfer to serving plates. Dust with icing sugar and decorate with mint sprigs. Serve with the vanilla-flavoured cream.

Note: The quantity of pastry is a little more than required for the pies. If preferred, the passion fruit filling can be cooked in a bain-marie, or heatproof bowl over a pan of simmering water, rather than in the microwave.

Lemon Syllabub

You will need to prepare the base for this syllabub a day in advance.

15-20 ml (3-4 tsp) sweet sherry
grated zest and juice of ½ large lemon
25 g (1 oz) caster sugar
200 ml (7 fl oz) double cream

To Decorate:
finely pared zest of ½ lemon, thinly shredded
5 ml (1 tsp) caster sugar

1 Place the sherry, grated lemon zest and juice, and the sugar in a jug. Stir until the sugar is dissolved, then cover and leave to stand overnight.

2 Transfer the sherry mixture to a large bowl. Add the cream and whip until fairly stiff. Spoon into two serving glasses. Chill in the refrigerator for 1-2 hours.

3 For the decoration, blanch the shredded lemon zest in a pan of boiling water for 30 seconds. Drain; dry on kitchen paper and toss in the caster sugar.

4 Arrange the frosted lemon shreds on top of the syllabubs to serve.

Macerated Minted Pineapple with Spiced Mascarpone

½ medium pineapple
300 ml (½ pint) pineapple juice
125 g (4 oz) caster sugar
22 ml (1½ tbsp) dark rum
15 ml (1 tbsp) lemon juice
30 ml (2 tbsp) shredded mint leaves

Spiced Mascarpone:
60 ml (4 tbsp) mascarpone
7.5 ml (1½ tsp) icing sugar
2.5 ml (½ tsp) ground cardamom

To Decorate:
mint leaves

1 Peel, core and slice the pineapple, making sure you remove all of the woody 'eyes'. Place the pineapple slices in a shallow dish.

2 Put the pineapple juice and sugar in a small heavy-based pan and stir over a low heat until the sugar is dissolved. Bring to the boil and simmer until the syrup is reduced by one third. Take off the heat and stir in the rum, lemon juice and shredded mint.

3 Pour the syrup over the pineapple slices and set aside to macerate for 1-2 hours, until ready to serve.

4 In the meantime, mix the mascarpone, icing sugar and ground cardamom together in a bowl.

5 To serve, transfer the pineapple slices to individual serving plates and drizzle over some of the minted syrup. Decorate with mint leaves and serve accompanied by the spiced mascarpone.

Strawberry Shortbread with Irish Chocolate Cream

Shortbread:
40 g (1½ oz) hazelnuts, toasted
25 g (1 oz) blanched almonds, toasted
75 g (3 oz) self-raising flour
75 g (3 oz) caster sugar
75 g (3 oz) butter

Filling:
50 ml (2 fl oz) thick double cream
1 mango, peeled, stoned and chopped
75 g (3 oz) strawberries, roughly chopped

Irish Chocolate Cream:
100 g (4 oz) good-quality plain chocolate, in pieces
2 eggs, separated
30 ml (2 tbsp) double cream
30 ml (2 tbsp) caster sugar
dash of Irish whisky

To Finish:
icing sugar, for dusting
grated chocolate, for sprinkling

1 To make the shortbread, put the hazelnuts and toasted almonds in a blender or food processor and whizz until finely chopped. Add the flour, sugar and butter and process until the mixture resembles fine breadcrumbs. Bring the dough together with one hand to form a ball and wrap in cling film. Chill in the refrigerator for approximately 30 minutes.

2 Meanwhile, make the Irish chocolate cream. Melt the chocolate in a bowl set over a pan of simmering water. Remove the bowl from the pan and let cool slightly, then beat in the egg yolks, using a wooden spoon. Stir in the cream. Whisk the egg whites in another bowl until they form peaks, add the sugar and continue to whisk until soft peaks form. Gently fold into the chocolate mixture, then add a dash of whisky to taste. Chill in the refrigerator for at least 30 minutes to firm up.

3 Roll out the shortbread dough thinly and cut out 6 rounds, using a 7.5 cm (3 inch) pastry cutter. Place on a baking sheet. Bake in a preheated oven at 200°C (400°F) mark 6 for approximately 8 minutes until golden. Leave on the baking sheet for 5 minutes, then transfer to a wire rack to cool.

4 Assemble the biscuits into two towers, sandwiching them together with the cream and half of the chopped fruit.

5 Purée the rest of the mango in a blender or food processor, pass through a sieve into a bowl and sweeten with a little icing sugar to taste, to make the mango coulis. Repeat with the remainder of the strawberries to make a strawberry coulis.

6 Carefully transfer the biscuit towers to individual serving plates and surround with the mango and strawberry coulis. Dust with icing sugar and sprinkle a little grated chocolate on top. Serve with the Irish chocolate cream.

Blackcurrant Mousse

175 g (6 oz) blackcurrants
25-50 g (1-2 oz) sugar, to taste
7 g (¼ oz/1½ tsp) powdered gelatine
45 ml (3 tbsp) water
90 ml (3 fl oz) double cream
2 egg whites

To Serve:
few blackcurrants and mint leaves, to
   decorate
Langue de Chat biscuits (see right)

1 Put the blackcurrants in a heavy-based pan with the sugar and cook over a low heat for 5-10 minutes until softened; let cool slightly. Transfer the blackcurrants to a blender or food processor and work to a purée. Pass through a sieve to remove the seeds; the purée should measure 120 ml (4 fl oz).

2 Sprinkle the gelatine over the 45 ml (3 tbsp) cold water in a bowl and leave to soften for 2-3 minutes, then stand the bowl over a pan of simmering water until the gelatine is dissolved.

3 Stir the blackcurrant purée into the dissolved gelatine and set aside to cool.

4 Lightly whip the cream in a bowl until it begins to hold its shape.

5 In a separate bowl, whisk the egg whites until stiff, but not dry.

6 Fold the cream into the blackcurrant mixture, then carefully fold this into the whisked egg whites. Pour into ramekins or other individual serving dishes and place in the refrigerator until set; about 2 hours.

7 Decorate the mousses with a few fresh blackcurrants and mint leaves. Serve with the langue de chat biscuits.

Langue de Chat Biscuits

50 g (2 oz) caster sugar
50 g (2 oz) butter
1-2 drops of vanilla essence
2 egg whites
50 g (2 oz) plain flour

1 Cream the sugar, butter and vanilla essence in a food processor until well blended.

2 Add the egg whites, a little at a time, then add the flour and process until smooth.

3 Put teaspoonfuls of the mixture on a baking sheet lined with non-stick baking parchment, spacing them well apart. Bake in a preheated oven at 220°C (425°F) mark 7 for 8 minutes.

4 Leave the biscuits on the baking sheet for a few minutes, then transfer to a wire rack to cool.

Note: This quantity makes about 8-12 biscuits, depending on size.

Lavender Brûlée

For this dessert the cream is infused a day in advance with the lavender and juniper berries.

300 ml (½ pint) single cream
8 stems of lavender flowers, chopped
3 juniper berries, crushed
3 egg yolks
55 g (2 oz) caster sugar
soft brown sugar, for sprinkling

1 Place the cream, chopped lavender and juniper berries in a deep microwave-proof bowl. Cover the bowl with perforated cling film and microwave on HIGH for 2 minutes. Leave to rest for 4 minutes.

2 Repeat this process twice more, watching very carefully during the final cooking time that the mixture does not boil. Allow to cool, then leave to infuse in the refrigerator overnight.

3 The next day, heat the infused cream again in the microwave to scalding point. Meanwhile, whisk the egg yolks and sugar together in a bowl. Gradually pour on the hot cream mixture, stirring continuously. Pass the mixture through a very fine sieve into a bowl, then pour into 2 ramekin dishes.

4 Stand the ramekins in a bain-marie (or roasting tin containing enough hot water to come halfway up the sides of the dishes). Cook in a preheated oven at 140°C (275°F) mark 1 for about 1 hour or until just set. Allow to cool, then chill in the refrigerator for about 1 hour.

5 Sprinkle a layer of brown sugar over the top of each crème and place under a preheated high grill until bubbling and caramelised. Leave to stand for 10-15 minutes before serving.

Note: Alternatively, use a blow torch to caramelise the sugar.

Triple Chocolate Mousse with Orange Cream Sauce

For optimum results, make sure you use top quality chocolate for the mousse.

Mousse:
12.5 ml (2½ tsp) powdered gelatine
37.5 ml (2½ tbsp) water
2 eggs
1 egg yolk
15 ml (1 tbsp) caster sugar
25 g (1 oz) milk chocolate
25 g (1 oz) white chocolate
25 g (1 oz) dark chocolate
150 ml (¼ pint) double cream

Sauce:
10 ml (2 tsp) preserving sugar
150 ml (¼ pint) double cream
grated zest of 1 orange
22 ml (1½ tbsp) orange juice

To Decorate:
physalis fruit or soft berry fruits

1 First make the sauce. Put the sugar and cream in a heavy-based saucepan. Bring to a simmer and simmer gently for 10-15 minutes until reduced to a thickened creamy consistency. Take off the heat, add the orange zest and juice, and stir gently. Pour into a small bowl, cover and refrigerate.

2 To make the mousse, sprinkle the gelatine over the water in a small heatproof bowl and leave to soften for 2-3 minutes.

3 Whisk the whole eggs, egg yolk and sugar together in a bowl, using an electric mixer, for about 6-8 minutes until very creamy.

4 Melt the different chocolates separately in 3 small heatproof bowls over pans of simmering water.

5 Stand the bowl containing the softened gelatine over a pan of simmering water to dissolve, then stir into the whisked egg mixture.

6 In a separate bowl, lightly whip the cream until it begins to hold its shape, then fold into the mousse mixture.

7 Divide the mixture equally between 3 bowls. Fold each different melted chocolate into a portion of the mousse mixture, so that you have a white mousse, a milk chocolate mousse and a dark mousse.

8 Line each of two 7.5 cm (3 inch) metal rings with a collar of greaseproof paper. Stand these on individual serving plates. First, pour in the milk chocolate mousse, dividing it equally between the rings. Cover with the white mixture, then top with the dark chocolate mousse. Place in the refrigerator for 1-2 hours, until set.

9 When set, carefully remove the metal rings and peel away the lining paper. Pour some orange sauce around one side of each mousse. Decorate with fruit.

Chocolate Mousse with Chocolate Truffles

Truffles:
50 g (2 oz) good-quality dark chocolate, in pieces
10 ml (2 tsp) double cream
5 ml (1 tsp) brandy
50 g (2 oz) icing sugar (approximately)

Mousse:
150 g (5 oz) good-quality dark chocolate
knob of butter
10 ml (2 tsp) water
2 eggs, separated
100 ml (3½ fl oz) double cream
15 ml (1 tbsp) Tia Maria

To Decorate:
a little whipped cream
grated plain chocolate, for sprinkling

1 First make the truffles. Melt 25 g (1 oz) of the chocolate in a heatproof bowl over a pan of simmering water. Take off the heat, then stir in the cream and brandy. Stir in the icing sugar gradually, until stiff enough to roll into balls.

2 Put the truffles on a plate, cover and place in the refrigerator for 30 minutes or until set.

3 To finish the truffles, melt the remaining 25 g (1 oz) chocolate (as above) and let cool slightly. Dip the truffles into the melted chocolate, turning them to coat all over. Chill in the refrigerator until required.

4 To make the mousse, melt the chocolate with a knob of butter and 10 ml (2 tsp) water in a heatproof bowl over a pan of simmering water. Take off the heat, let cool slightly then mix in the egg yolks.

5 Whip the cream in a separate bowl until soft peaks form, then fold into the chocolate mixture. Add the Tia Maria.

6 In a clean bowl, whisk the egg whites until stiff, then carefully fold the chocolate mixture into the egg whites.

7 Pour the mousse into two coffee cups and chill in the refrigerator for 1-2 hours.

8 When required, decorate the mousses with whipped cream and a little grated chocolate. Serve accompanied by the chocolate truffles.

Pistachio Praline Islands floating on a Custard Sauce

Praline:
50 g (2 oz) caster sugar
50 g (2 oz) shelled pistachio nuts, roughly broken into pieces

Custard Sauce:
2 egg yolks
50 g (2 oz) caster sugar
150 ml (¼ pint) milk
150 ml (¼ pint) single cream
pinch of freshly grated nutmeg

Meringues:
2 egg whites
75 g (3 oz) caster sugar

To Decorate:
mint sprigs

1 To make the praline, put the sugar in a heavy-based saucepan over a gentle heat and stir with a metal spoon until the sugar melts and begins to caramelise. Continue to cook, without stirring, to a deep brown caramel. Carefully add the broken pistachios, then pour the mixture onto an oiled baking sheet. Leave to cool and harden.

2 Meanwhile, make the custard sauce. Place the egg yolks and sugar in a heavy-based saucepan and gradually whisk in the milk and single cream. Continue to whisk over a very low heat until you have a smooth custard that is thick enough to coat the back of a wooden spoon; do not allow to boil. Flavour with a pinch of nutmeg. Immediately strain into two serving dishes and leave to cool.

3 Roughly crush the praline into small pieces; set aside one third for decoration.

4 To make the meringues, whisk the egg whites in a bowl until stiff. Gradually whisk in the caster sugar, a spoonful at a time, until the mixture is stiff and shiny. Fold in two thirds of the crushed praline.

5 Place tablespoonfuls of the meringue mixture on a baking tray lined with non-stick baking parchment. Cook in the middle of a preheated oven at 130°C (260°F) mark ½-1 for about 50 minutes or until the meringues are pale golden and crispy on the outside with 'gooey' pieces of praline in the middle. Allow to cool.

6 To serve, float 2 or 3 meringue 'islands' on each portion of custard sauce. Decorate with the reserved praline and sprigs of mint. Serve at once.

Summer Fruit Sorbet with a Raspberry Coulis

225 g (8 oz) mixed frozen summer berries
  (eg strawberries, raspberries, blackberries)
½ large or 1 small banana
45-60 ml (3-4 tbsp) icing sugar, to taste
about 60 ml (2 fl oz) kirsch
100 g (4 oz) fresh raspberries
30 ml (2 tbsp) double cream

To Decorate:
icing sugar, for dusting
grated plain chocolate, for sprinkling
mint leaves
few raspberries

To Serve:
langue de chat biscuits

1 To make the sorbet, purée the frozen fruit with the banana, 30 ml (2 tbsp) icing sugar and a dash of kirsch. Divide between two or three individual fluted freezer-proof dishes and place in the freezer for at least 1 hour, until firm.

2 To make the coulis, purée the fresh raspberries in a blender or food processor, then pass through a sieve into a bowl to remove the pips. Add icing sugar to taste and stir in a generous dash of kirsch.

3 To serve, turn out the sorbet onto individual serving plates. Surround with the raspberry coulis, dot with the cream and feather with a skewer. Dust with icing sugar and sprinkle with grated chocolate. Decorate with mint leaves and raspberries. Serve at once with langue de chat biscuits.

Note: This recipe serves 2-3.

Marmalade Ice Cream in a Chocolate Cage with a Bitter Orange Sauce

Ice Cream:
150 ml (¼ pint) double cream
90 ml (3 fl oz) skimmed milk
2 egg yolks
50 g (2 oz) caster sugar
25 ml (5 tsp) marmalade (preferably homemade)

Sauce:
30 ml (2 tbsp) caster sugar
finely grated zest and juice of 2 oranges
7.5 ml (1½ tsp) Cointreau
50 g (2 oz) marmalade (preferably homemade)

To Finish:
50 g (2 oz) good-quality plain chocolate

1 To make the ice cream, pour the cream and milk into a heavy-based saucepan and slowly bring to the boil. Meanwhile, whisk the egg yolks and sugar together in a bowl. Slowly pour the hot cream mixture onto the egg mixture, whisking constantly. Return to the saucepan and stir in the marmalade. Stir over a low heat until the custard is slightly thickened – just enough to coat the back of the wooden spoon; do not allow to boil.

2 Pour into a chilled bowl and allow to cool, then transfer to an ice-cream maker and churn for about 20 minutes until firm.

3 To make the sauce, put the sugar in a heavy-based pan over a low heat until melted. Increase the heat slightly to medium and cook, without stirring, for about 1-2 minutes until you have a golden brown caramel. Take off the heat and carefully add the orange zest and juice, liqueur and marmalade. Stir until smooth, then return to the heat and bring to the boil. Simmer gently for 5-10 minutes until the sauce is reduced and shiny.

4 To serve, melt the chocolate in a bowl over a pan of simmering water; let cool slightly. Put the melted chocolate into a greaseproof paper piping bag. Scoop a portion of ice cream onto the middle of each serving plate. Pipe melted chocolate over the ice cream to form a 'cage'; it will set on contact with the ice cream. Surround with the warm orange sauce and serve immediately.

Praline Mascarpone Ice Cream with Sautéed Apricots

Sautéed Apricots:
6 no-need-to-soak dried apricots
300 ml (½ pint) freshly made hot tea
25 g (1 oz) vanilla sugar
knob of butter

Ice Cream:
50 g (2 oz) caster sugar
50 g (2 oz) blanched almonds
220 g (7½ oz) can condensed milk
125 g (4 oz) mascarpone cheese

To Serve:
Almond Tuiles (see right)

1 Put the apricots in a bowl, pour on the hot tea and leave to soak overnight.

2 To make the praline, put the caster sugar and almonds in a small heavy-based pan. Heat gently, stirring occasionally, until the sugar is melted. Continue cooking to a golden brown caramel, or until a sugar thermometer registers 165°C (330°F). Immediately remove from the heat and pour onto an oiled baking tray. Leave to cool and harden, then grind to a fine powder in a food processor or blender.

3 To make the ice cream, put the condensed milk, mascarpone and praline in an ice-cream maker. Churn for about 20 minutes, until firm.

4 Meanwhile, drain the apricots, reserving the tea. Put the tea in a saucepan with the vanilla sugar and dissolve over a low heat, then increase the heat and boil until well reduced and syrupy.

5 Melt the butter in a small pan, add the apricots and sauté until lightly browned. Add the tea syrup and cook gently for 5-8 minutes.

6 To serve, scoop the ice cream onto individual serving plates, spoon the hot apricots in syrup alongside and serve at once, with the almond tuiles.

Almond Tuiles

75 g (3 oz) butter
75 g (3 oz) caster sugar
50 g (2 oz) plain flour
pinch of salt
75 g (3 oz) flaked almonds, finely shredded

1 Cream the butter and sugar together in a bowl until light and fluffy.

2 Sift the flour and salt together over the mixture. Add the shredded almonds and mix until evenly blended.

3 Place 2-3 heaped teaspoonfuls of the mixture on a greased baking sheet, spacing them well apart; flatten with the back of a damp fork. Bake in a preheated oven at 200°C (400°F) mark 6 for 6-8 minutes.

4 Leave on the baking sheet for about 30 seconds, then carefully lift off, using a palette knife. Place each biscuit over a greased rolling pin to curve and leave to cool. Once firm, carefully lift off the tuiles and place on a wire rack.

Note: This quantity makes about 8 tuiles. To ensure they do not harden before you have time to shape them, bake only 2 or 3 at a time.

Brandy Snap Baskets filled with Stem Ginger Ice Cream

Brandy Snap Baskets:
25 g (1 oz) unsalted butter
40 g (1½ oz) caster sugar
2.5 ml (½ tsp) ground ginger
22 ml (1½ tbsp) golden syrup
25 g (1 oz) plain flour, sifted

Ice Cream:
150 ml (¼ pint) milk
1 vanilla pod, split
2 egg yolks
50 g (2 oz) caster sugar
150 ml (¼ pint) double cream
2 pieces preserved stem ginger in syrup

To Decorate:
mint leaves

1 To make the brandy snap baskets, put the butter, sugar, ground ginger and golden syrup in a heavy-based pan and heat slowly until the butter is melted and the sugar dissolved. Take off the heat and allow to cool. Stir the flour into the cooled melted mixture and mix until smooth.

2 Place teaspoonfuls of the mixture on 2 baking sheets lined with non-stick baking parchment, spacing them well apart. Bake in a preheated oven at 180°C (350°F) mark 4 for approximately 7 minutes.

3 Leave on the baking sheets for 20 seconds until slightly cooled, then remove with a palette knife and lay each one over a suitable mould, such as an individual pudding basin or an orange. Shape to form baskets, then allow to cool. When firm, carefully lift off the baskets.

4 To make the ice cream, pour the milk into a heavy-based saucepan, add the vanilla pod and slowly bring to the boil.

Remove from the heat and leave to infuse for about 10 minutes.

5 Beat the egg yolks and sugar together in a bowl until pale and creamy. Heat the milk to just below boiling, then gradually pour half of it on to the beaten egg mixture, whisking constantly.

6 Return to the pan containing the remaining milk and heat very slowly, stirring all the time, until thickened enough to coat the back of the wooden spoon; do not allow to boil. Turn into a chilled bowl and allow to cool.

7 When cold, stir in the cream and remove the vanilla pod. Transfer to an ice-cream maker and churn until thickened. Finely chop 1½ pieces of the stem ginger, add to the ice cream and churn until firm. Turn into a freezerproof container and freeze until required.

8 To serve, place a brandy snap basket on each serving plate and fill with scoops of ice cream. Decorate with mint leaves and the reserved stem ginger.

Notes: The above quantities make about 8 brandy snap baskets. Store in an airtight tin and use as required.

If the biscuits become too firm to shape, return the baking sheet to the oven for 20-30 seconds to soften the mixture slightly.

Brandy Snap Coffee Cup filled with Rum and Cappuccino Ice Cream

Brandy Snap Cups:
50 g (2 oz) butter
50 g (2 oz) granulated sugar
65 g (2½ oz) golden syrup
50 g (2 oz) plain flour
15 ml (1 tbsp) ground ginger
30 ml (2 tbsp) lemon juice

Ice Cream:
3 egg yolks
75 g (3 oz) icing sugar
75 ml (5 tbsp) strong black coffee, cooled
15 ml (1 tbsp) rum
5 ml (1 tsp) vanilla essence
375 ml (13 fl oz) double cream, lightly
   whipped

To Serve:
60 ml (4 tbsp) double cream, whipped
5 ml (1 tsp) rum, to taste
chocolate-coated coffee beans, to decorate

1 To make the brandy snap cups, put the butter, sugar and syrup into a small heavy-based pan and stir over a low heat until melted and evenly blended. Meanwhile, sift the flour and ginger together into a bowl. Make a well in the centre and add the syrup mixture. Stir well and mix in the lemon juice.

2 To make the 'brandy snap saucers', place two tablespoonfuls of the mixture on a greased baking sheet, spacing them well apart to allow for spreading. Bake in a preheated oven at 170°C (325°F) mark 3 for 8 minutes. Leave on the baking sheet for a few seconds, then quickly transfer to two greased saucers, about 20 cm (8 inches) in diameter. Leave for 3-5 minutes to firm up, then carefully transfer to a wire rack.

3 To make the cups, spread the remaining mixture into two oblongs, each approximately 2 x 5 cm (¾ x 2 inches), on a greased baking sheet, spacing them well apart to allow for spreading. Bake in the oven for 8-10 minutes until golden. Leave on the baking sheet for a few seconds, then trim to neat oblongs, about 20 x 25 cm (8 x 10 inches). Roll around greased rolling pins, overlapping the edges to form cylinders. Hold in position for 20-30 seconds until firm, then carefully remove.

4 To make the ice cream, whisk the egg yolks and icing sugar together in a bowl until pale and creamy. Stir in the remaining ingredients until evenly blended, then transfer to an ice-cream maker and churn for about 20 minutes until firm.

5 To serve, position the brandy snap cups on their saucers and fill with scoops of the ice cream. Flavour the whipped cream with rum to taste and add a spoonful to each dessert. Decorate with the coffee beans.

Banana Bombe with a Mango Sauce

Ice Cream:
1 banana
200 g (7 oz) condensed milk
150 ml (¼ pint) thick single cream

Bombe:
60 ml (4 tbsp) granulated sugar
15 ml (1 tbsp) water

Sauce:
½ ripe mango
juice of ½ lime

To Serve:
Cigarette Russe (see right)

1 To make the ice cream, mash the banana in a bowl until smooth. Whisk in the condensed milk, followed by the single cream. Transfer the mixture to an ice-cream maker and churn until frozen.

2 For the bombes, put the sugar and water into a small heavy-based pan and heat gently until dissolved. Increase the heat and cook steadily to a light caramel, ie the syrup registers 160°C (320°F) on a sugar thermometer. Take off the heat and dip the base of the pan briefly into cold water to stop cooking.

3 Oil two upturned round-based metal bowls or ladles. Using a tablespoon, drizzle threads of caramel back and forth all over the oiled surface in a criss-cross pattern to form a cage. Drizzle a trail of caramel around the edge of the mould to form the rim of the cage. Allow to cool until set hard, then carefully loosen the caramel cage and lift off.

4 For the sauce, peel and roughly chop the mango, then put into a food processor or blender with the lime juice. Work to a purée, then pass through a sieve to ensure a smooth result.

5 To serve, place a caramel cage on each serving plate and fill with scoops of ice cream. Surround with the mango sauce and serve accompanied by the biscuits.

Cigarette Russe

2 egg whites
100 g (4 oz) caster sugar
50 g (2 oz) butter, melted
50 g (2 oz) plain flour, sifted
2-3 drops of vanilla essence

1 Lightly whisk the egg whites in a bowl until foamy, then whisk in the sugar until smooth. Stir in the cooled, melted butter, flour and vanilla essence, until evenly incorporated and smooth.

2 Spoon the mixture into oblongs, about 7.5 x 5 cm (3 x 2 inches), on baking sheets lined with non-stick baking parchment, two per baking sheet.

3 Bake, one sheet at a time, in a pre-heated oven at 200°C (400°F) mark 6 for 5-6 minutes until golden brown. Let stand for a second or two, then carefully lift off using a fish slice. Wrap each one around a greased wooden spoon handle.

4 Let cool slightly until firm, then carefully ease the biscuits off the handles and transfer to a wire rack to cool.

Menus

Claire Howell's Menu

Main Course
Lamb's Liver with Melted Onion and Marsala (p45)
Sliced Potatoes baked with Tomatoes and Basil (p78)

Dessert
Hot Raspberry Soufflé, served with
a Warm Raspberry Coulis (p94)

Thomas Stephens' Menu

Main Course
Crispy Roast Duck Breast with Cranberry and Orange Sauce (p31)
Potato and Apple Rösti (p67)
Glazed Carrots
Sugar Snap Peas

Dessert
Lemon Meringue Roulade (p102)

Philip Fanning's Menu

Main Course
Barbary Duck with Mango and Damson Sauce (p30)
Crunchy-topped Leeks (p62)
Glazed Carrots
Scalloped Potatoes (p75)

Dessert
Autumn Fruit Tarte Tatin with Blackberry Ice Cream (p95)

Helen Elliott's Menu

Main Course

Poached Fillet of Salmon with a Lime and Ginger Sauce (p10)
Layered Vegetables (p59)
Almond Potatoes (p76)

Dessert

Blackberries under a blanket of Lemon Syllabub (p109)
Langue de Chat (p109)

Sara Kent's Menu

Main Course

Poached Fillet of Beef in a Madeira Sauce (p36)
Potato Gratin (p77)
Mixed Pepper Stir-fry (p62)

Dessert

Summer Fruit Sorbet with a Raspberry Coulis (p119)
Langue de Chat Biscuits

Claire Kent's Menu

Main Course

Chicken Breast stuffed with Peppers (p24)
Stir-fried Vegetable Bundles (p57)
Potato and Parsnip Rösti (p68)

Dessert

Toffee Pecan Nut Cheesecake with Butterscotch Sauce (p103)

Annie Stradling's Menu

Main Course

Steamed Pork Roll with Tomato and Pepper Stuffing (p47)

Potato Rösti (p69)

Ratatouille (p58)

Dessert

Lemon Tart with a Raspberry Coulis (p97)

Georgina Wolsey's Menu

Main Course

Pan-fried Swordfish Steak on a bed of Marinated Aubergine with a Warm Lemon Dressing (p15)

Potatoes flavoured with Saffron

Dessert

Chocolate and Walnut Tart, served with a Rhubarb and Raspberry Compote and Orange Liqueur Cream (p96)

Courtney Smyth's Menu

Main Course

Spicy Lamb Kebab (p42)

Courgette and Feta Pitta (p43)

Minted Mustardy Potato and Peas (p70)

Tabouleh (p84)

Dessert

Passion Fruit Delight with Fragrant Cream (p110)

Tanya Bradshaw's Menu

Main Course

Skate Fillet stuffed with Air-dried Ham, served with
a Red Pepper Sauce (p19)
Timbale of Mixed Rice (p83)
Citrus Leeks with Sugar Snap Peas (p61)

Dessert

Mango Tarte Tatin, served with
Cinnamon Crème Fraîche (p98)

Alice Broad's Menu

Main Course

Wiltshire Ham, served with a Mushroom and
Madeira Sauce (p50)
Creamed Spinach with Nutmeg (p63)
Isosceles Roast Potatoes (p71)

Dessert

Baked Stuffed Apple with a Cranberry and Orange Sauce (p86)

Harriet Thomas' Menu

Main Course

Garlic and Honey Pork (p46)
Vegetable Noodles (p60)

Dessert

Grilled Banana with Cardamom Butter, served with
Vanilla Ice Cream (p87)

Chris Tonner's Menu

Main Course

*Pan-fried Turbot on a bed of Caramelised Shallots with
a Beurre Blanc Sauce (p16)*

Turned Vegetables

Dessert

Poached Citrus Pears (p107)

Calli Robertson's Menu

Main Course

*Medallions of Lamb and Pigeon Timbales on Potato Rösti with
Wild Mushrooms and a Lamb Jus (p44)*

Dessert

Wild Berries with Grand Marnier Cream and Shortbread (p108)

Courtney Lewis' Menu

Main Course

Salmon in a White Wine, Cucumber and Dill Sauce (p13)

Champ (p72)

Roasted Baby Plum Tomatoes

Dessert

*Mascarpone and Fromage Frais Cheesecake, served with
a Raspberry Coulis (p104)*

Jojo Lea's Menu

Main Course

Wild Duck Breast with Blackberry Sauce (p32)

Herby Duchesse Potatoes

Glazed Carrots

French Beans

Dessert

Triple Chocolate Mousse with Orange Cream Sauce (p116)

Alex Hicklin's Menu

Main Course

Medley of Sea Food on a bed of Spinach with Deep-fried Carrot Julienne and Steamed Potatoes, served with a Tarragon Dressing (p21)

Dessert

Pistachio Praline Islands floating on a Custard Sauce (p118)

Felicity Oswald's Menu

Main Course

Grilled Turmeric Chicken, served with a Watercress Sauce (p25)

Basil-fried Potato Balls (p73)

Garlic Acorn Squash (p66)

Dessert

*Steamed Chocolate Pudding, served with a
Rich Chocolate Sauce (p88)*

Katie Mitchell's Menu

Main Course

*Sea Bass with a Basil and Pine Nut Crust, served with
a Parsley Sauce (p17)*

Griddled Cherry Tomatoes

Dessert

*Marmalade Ice Cream in a Chocolate Cage with
a Bitter Orange Sauce (p120)*

Michelle Frankgate's Menu

Main Course

*Tranche of Cod Viennoise, served with
a Thai Seafood Sauce (p18)*

Spinach

New Potatoes

Dessert

Pear and Calvados Crumble, served with a Crème Anglais (p91)

Victoria Bowman's Menu

Main Course

Spiced Carrot Tart with Sweet Potato Pastry (p52)

Stir-fried Vegetables (p55)

Dessert

Lemon Syllabub (p111)

Andrew Stone's Menu

Main Course
Vanilla Roasted Duck with Honey Roast Root Vegetables (p33)

Dessert
*Bramley Apple Soufflé, with Calvados Cream
and Caramelised Apple (p92)*

Serena Martin's Menu

Main Course
*Salmon Fillet with a Sun-dried Tomato, Basil and
Cream Sauce (p11)*
Stir-fried Sugar Snap Peas and Cucumber (p54)
New Potatoes

Dessert
Chocolate Mousse with Chocolate Truffles (p117)

Luke Temple's Menu

Main Course
*Marinated Seared Thai Salmon in a Ginger and Teriyaki Sauce with
a Sweet Ginger Relish (p12)*
Caramelised Roasted Garlic Spinach (p63)
Japanese Rice (p82)

Dessert
*Mango Meringue Chinchilla with Coconut and
Chilli Ice Cream (p105)*

Elaine Alderson's Menu

Main Course

Rack of Lamb with a Wild Berry, Mint and Herb Sauce (p37)

Dauphinoise Potatoes (p79)

Purée of Parsnips (p66)

Dessert

*Fresh Fruit Fettucini with a Summer Fruit Medley and
Cassis Coulis, served with Clotted Cream (p93)*

Emily Botham's Menu

Main Course

*Peppered Swordfish on a bed of Camargue Rice with
a Thai Sauce and Sweet Potato Crisps (p14)*

Lamb's Leaf Salad with a Raspberry Vinaigrette (p54)

Dessert

Banana Bombe with a Mango Sauce (p124)

Cigarette Russe (p124)

Gary May's Menu

Main Course

Chicken Risotto with Mushrooms and Tomato (p29)

Dessert

Poached Pear with Butterscotch Sauce (p106)

Semi-Final Menu

Main Course

*Breast of Chicken stuffed with Wild Mushroom Forcemeat, served with
Pan-fried Chicken Livers and a Honey, Caraway and Cumin Sauce (p26)*

Saffron Potatoes

Julienne of Vegetables

Dessert

*Shortbread Tartlet filled with a Rich Chocolate Mousse,
served with Coffee and Almond Creams (p100)*

Semi-Final Menu

Main Course

*Bacon-wrapped Pork Tenderloin filled with Pine Nuts,
Sun-dried Tomatoes and Mushrooms (p49)*

Stir-fried Winter Vegetables

Creamed Potato Swirls with Herbs and Parmesan (p81)

Dessert

Ginger and Apricot Baked Alaska with an Orange and Apricot Coulis (p101)

Semi-Final Menu

Main Course

*Pan-fried Lamb Cutlets with a Parmesan Crust, served with
a Creamy Pesto Sauce (p38)*

Mustardy Baked Potatoes with Olives (p80)

Shredded Steamed Green Vegetables

Dessert

Macerated Minted Pineapple with Spiced Mascarpone (p112)

Semi-Final Menu

Main Course

Fillet of Lamb with a Port and Rosemary Sauce (p39)

Mushroom Medley (p64)

New Potatoes

Steamed Patty Pan Squash

Dessert

Brandy Snap Basket filled with Stem Ginger Ice Cream (p122)

Semi-Final Menu

Main Course

Lamb Brochette with Spiced Chutney (p40)

Mashed Potato flavoured with Olive Oil and Basil

Dessert

Lavender Brûlée (p115)

Semi-Final Menu

Main Course

*Chicken Breast filled with Courgette and Pistachio Nut Stuffing,
served with Red Pepper Sauce (p27)*

Stir-fried Green Vegetables

Individual Dauphinoise Potatoes (p80)

Dessert

Chocolate Puddle Pudding (p89)

Semi-Final Menu

Main Course

Braised Loin of Lamb with Cranberry Chutney and Crispy Onions (p41)

Root Vegetable Mash (p65)

Curly Kale with Sesame Seeds (p64)

Dessert

Praline Mascarpone Ice Cream with Sautéed Apricots (p121)

Almond Tuiles (p121)

Semi-Final Menu

Main Course

Cidered Fillet of Pork with Garlic and Sage (p48)

Dressed Baby Carrots, Leeks and Mangetout (p56)

Potato Nest (p74)

Dessert

Strawberry Shortbread with Irish Chocolate Cream (p113)

Semi-Final Menu

Main Course

Sautéed Chicken stuffed with Pine Nuts and Apricots on
a bed of Stir-fried Leek and Bacon (p28)

Baby Carrots

Roast Parsnips

Parisian Potatoes

Fine Green Beans

Dessert

Brandy Snap Coffee Cup filled with Rum and Cappuccino
Ice Cream (p123)

Final Menu

Main Course

Smoked Haddock with a Lemon and Cream Sauce (p20)

Colcannon (p67)

Dessert

Blueberry Mango Tartlet with Strawberry Sauce (p99)

Final Menu

Main Course

Pheasant Breast with Brandy and Cream Sauce (p34)

Celeriac and Apple Purée (p65)

Mixed Leaf Salad

Dessert

Blackcurrant Mousse (p114)

Langue de Chat Biscuits (p114)

Final Menu

Main Course

Seafood Roulade, with a Lime and Watercress Hollandaise (p22)

Rice Noodles with Shiitake Mushrooms and Oyster Sauce (p82)

Stir-fried Mixed Vegetables

Dessert

Baked Camellia Pudding with a Raspberry Sauce (p90)

The 1998 Junior MasterChef Judges

Chefs

Alastair Little

Thane Prince

Graeme Allen

Alison Yetman

James Martin

Robbie Millar

Roz Denny

Clive Dixon

Aaron Patterson

Antony Worrall Thompson

Ross Burden

Maddalena Bonino

Raymond Blanc

Celebrities

Anneka Rice

Ian McCaskill

Magenta De Vine

Alan Titchmarsh

Keith Barron

Sharron Davies

Roger Griffiths

Michael Ball

Sally Gunnell

Jenny Powell

Sue Lawley

Alan Coren

Prue Leith

Index